DISCOVERING PRICES

KENNETH J. ARROW LECTURE SERIES

KENNETH J. ARROW LECTURE SERIES

Kenneth J. Arrow's work has so deeply shaped the course of economics for the past sixty years that, in a sense, every modern economist is his student. His ideas, style of research, and breadth of vision have been a model for generations of the boldest, most creative, and most innovative economists. His work has yielded seminal theorems in areas such as general equilibrium theory, social choice theory, and endogenous growth theory, proving that simple ideas have profound effects. The Kenneth J. Arrow Lecture Series highlights economists from Nobel laureates to groundbreaking younger scholars, whose work builds on Arrow's scholarship as well as his innovative spirit. The books in the series are an expansion of the lectures that are held in Arrow's honor at Columbia University.

The lectures have been supported by Columbia University's Committee on Global Thought, Program for Economic Research, Center on Global Economic Governance, and Initiative for Policy Dialogue.

Creating a Learning Society: A New Approach to Growth, Development, and Social Progress, Joseph E. Stiglitz and Bruce C. Greenwald

The Arrow Impossibility Theorem, Eric Maskin and Amartya Sen

Speculation, Trading, and Bubbles, José A. Scheinkman

Moral Hazard in Health Insurance, Amy Finkelstein

Creating a Learning Society: A New Approach to Growth, Development, and Social Progress, Reader's Edition, Joseph E. Stiglitz and Bruce C. Greenwald

DISCOVERING PRICES

AUCTION DESIGN IN MARKETS WITH COMPLEX CONSTRAINTS

PAUL MILGROM

COLUMBIA UNIVERSITY PRESS
NEW YORK

Columbia University Press
Publishers Since 1893
New York Chichester, West Sussex
cup.columbia.edu

Paperback edition, 2021

Library of Congress Cataloging-in-Publication Data
Names: Milgrom, Paul R. (Paul Robert), 1948- author.
Title: Discovering prices : auction design in markets with complex constraints / Paul Milgrom.
Description: New York : Columbia University Press, 2017. | Series: Kenneth J.
Arrow lecture series | Includes bibliographical references and index.
Identifiers: LCCN 2016046839 (print) | LCCN 2017003117 (ebook) |
ISBN 9780231175982 (cloth) | ISBN 9780231175999 (pbk.) |
ISBN 9780231544573 (electronic)
Subjects: LCSH: Auctions—Mathematical models. |
Auction theory. | Prices—Mathematical models.
Classification: LCC HF5476 .M549 2017 (print) |
LCC HF5476 (ebook) | DDC 381/.1701—dc23
LC record available at https://lccn.loc.gov/2016046839

Cover design: Noah Arlow

For Eva forever

CONTENTS

PREFACE

This monograph expands on a lecture honoring Kenneth Arrow that I delivered at Columbia University on November 17, 2014. My mandate was to give a lecture building upon one of Arrow's many contributions to economics; an easy task, since his theorizing has carved such a broad path within economics. Previous lecturers had spoken about welfare economics and social choice theory, health economics, the economics of innovation, financial economics, and much more.

This monograph is inspired in part by a different area of Ken's work, which focuses on general equilibrium theory and the associated price-determination processes. As traditionally conceived, general equilibrium theory develops some of the oldest ideas in economics, dating back to Adam Smith. Was Smith right to think that prices can be used to guide resource allocation, even when there is a vast array of different goods? Can the famous "invisible hand" of the market help buyers and seller discover market-clearing prices—ones at which supply and demand are in perfect balance?

In the neoclassical tradition of general equilibrium theory to which Arrow contributed, these questions were posed within particular formal models. In those, the products for which prices would be quoted are part of the formulation. No attention is paid to why those particular products are the ones the economy is trading. Much of the analysis also supposes that goods are divisible (roughly true for units of sugar and rice, but less so for cars and houses) and that production takes no advantage of economies of scale. Further, in nearly all such models, only two kinds of constraints are acknowledged: resource constraints, limiting demand not to exceed supply, and sometimes incentive constraints, ensuring that participants are willing both to provide accurate planning information and to follow the dictates of the resulting plan. Given hypothetical markets satisfying these assumptions, the models are used to pose questions about the efficiency or inefficiency of equilibrium. The answers that are true in the formal model inform our understanding of real markets.

In recent years, a very different approach to the study of prices and decentralized systems has begun to develop among computer scientists. It focuses on a set of issues that economic models mostly push aside. One is that discovering efficient resource allocations could require unrealistically vast amounts of communication among participants, challenging the capacity even of modern communications channels. A second is that, even if all the necessary information were available, computing efficient allocations might take too much time, even on very fast computers. In these models, there may be scale economies, and prices that clear all the markets may not exist. In markets that look like that, it can be important to have communications systems and algorithms that are simple, run very fast, and provide good approximations of efficient resource allocations. "Simple," "fast," and "approximate" are words one rarely encounters in traditional economic theories.

The economic and computer science issues come together for me in my own work helping the U.S. government to arrange for certain bands of radio spectrum to be moved away from broadcast television and into mobile broadband. This work has provided me with an opportunity to honor Arrow by writing, as he often did, at a boundary between two disciplines. Inspired by Arrow's own writing, I seek to tackle a set of problems not by formulating them narrowly to fit into an existing conceptual framework of economics but by following them where they lead, as needed to provide an actual, working solution. In my analysis, one particular idea that Arrow emphasized has a featured role. His analysis of gross substitutes and its role in guiding dynamic price adjustments morphs, in this monograph, into an analysis of how an auction-based system can be used to guide certain complex resource-allocation problems and to find associated prices.

In preparing this monograph, I benefited from support and advice from many sources. My research was supported in part by a grant from the National Science Foundation. My discussants at Columbia included Arrow himself, along with Patrick Bolton, Joseph Stiglitz, and Jay Sethuraman. I thank all of these people for the insights they offered. At Stanford, several students and colleagues worked with me to help make my writing clearer, improve notation, correct errors, and ensure that the book would be approachable.

For these invaluable services, I thank Mohammad Akbarpour, Piotr Dworczak, Ricardo de la O Flores, Sidhanth Grover, Alexa Lea Haushalter, Xiaoning Liu, Zheng Ma, Marion Ott, Megan Rose McCann, Erling Skancke, Inbal Talgam-Cohen, Andrew Vogt, and Daniel Layton Wright. Finally, I thank the editors at Columbia University Press, especially Bridget Flannery-McCoy, for their assistance throughout the process.

DISCOVERING PRICES

1

INTRODUCTION

The mid-1990s was an auspicious time for the new academic discipline that was soon to become known as "market design." This period saw the introduction of the first Internet Web browser, which provided consumers easy access to the World Wide Web and, soon after, to vast volumes of Web-based commerce. Online auctions like eBay, online stores and marketplaces like Amazon, and instantaneous advertising auctions like those run by Google emerged, and automation required that these markets operate with formal rules. These companies and others hired economists—who were thought to understand how markets actually work—to help engineers and programmers in designing the necessary rules.

Web-based companies were not the only ones looking for advice about how their markets should be organized. The same time period also saw the redesign of the National Resident Matching Program (NRMP). That program operates the market to match newly graduating doctors to hospital residency programs in the United States. The traditional matching algorithm, which had worked well for four decades, began by asking each hospital to rank the doctors who might enter its residency program and each doctor to rank the hospitals. In the usual mathematical model, those preferences are real things that doctors and hospitals know. According to that model, the NRMP system for determining matches between doctors and hospitals encouraged honest preference reporting and led to matches that were "stable," meaning that there is no doctor and hospital who would both prefer to make a new deal with each other rather than to honor the one recommended by the match. But the model is not an exact match for reality, and one important omission became apparent only in the 1990s. What changed was the number of women in medical schools. Increasingly, graduating doctors were married to other doctors, and the couples insisted on compatible placements. The old system was not designed to accommodate that. Economists found themselves deeply engaged in new research about devising a new, replacement system that would have similar theoretical properties while still accommodating the needs of couples, in addition to the needs of single doctors and hospitals.

During the same period, the first U.S. auction of licenses to use radio spectrum to support services like pagers and mobile phones took place. These auctions, too, were designed with help and guidance from academic economists. There were thousands of licenses to be allocated, each described by the geographic area that it covered and the frequencies that it used. No two licenses were quite the same, but some buyers regarded certain licenses as *economic substitutes*—meaning roughly that the buyer would be less eager to acquire one license if it knew it could acquire the other more cheaply—and some buyers regarded certain licenses as *economic complements*—meaning that a buyer would be willing to pay a premium to acquire both licenses. In the absence of complements, the economic problem of efficiently assigning licenses to companies is similar to the problem of assigning single doctors to hospitals, but the possibility of complements makes the problem much more complex. Indeed, the doctors in a married couple would usually be willing to pay a premium (by accepting a lesser placement) if the two jobs were at the same or nearby hospitals. In both medical matching and license auctions, the presence of complements was what made the redesign of the market so challenging.

Despite all this practical activity, some economists schooled in traditional economic theory were skeptical of the field of market design altogether. Why, many asked, would markets need designing? Why can unregulated market participants not take care of themselves? According to a view that is still espoused by many economists, if resources are allocated in an inefficient way, and if parties can negotiate freely among themselves without artificially imposed constraints, then the parties will be sufficiently motivated to alleviate and eventually eliminate any important inefficiency without any outside assistance. According to that view, no organized market is needed to promote efficient trade.

This strongly held belief in the power of unregulated markets was baked into the formal models economists traditionally used to understand the world. Formal claims in economics are often presented in mathematical terms as theorems that are based on the assumptions of a particular mathematical model. Formalization is important to economics, because it allows readers and others to identify the precise assumptions that underpin any purported conclusion, to verify that the assumptions really do imply this conclusion, and to check how deviations from the assumptions might alter the conclusion. In the case of the traditional view described earlier, the relevant claim is known as the *Coase theorem*, named for its originator, British economist Ronald Coase. The theorem relies on four assumptions about the parties involved in any transaction: that they have secure, transferable property rights; can bargain freely and effectively; can transact without costs or regulatory constraints; and will transact whenever it is mutually beneficial to do so. Most important from Coase's perspective was that the efficiency of the outcome does not depend on who initially owns any property rights, because ownership can be changed, if necessary, as part of the bargain.

Coase understood that this model would not apply exactly to any real situation, so the legal default situation could be important in practice. Many barriers to securing property rights and making them transferable, bargaining effectively, making and enforcing contracts, and conducting trade often stand in the way. In a straightforward bargain between two people, the conclusion described by the Coase theorem might be reasonably realistic. But bargaining is especially difficult when an agreement among multiple parties is needed to achieve much benefit, and the conclusion of the theorem is therefore least likely to describe real outcomes in such cases. Despite these qualifications, reasoning along "Coasian" lines bolstered a deeply held belief among many economists that regulations on markets should be minimal and that market participants are usually best left to take care of their own affairs, without being subjected to "designs" imposed by regulators or, certainly, by academic economists.

Long before Coase, an even older strand known as classical economic theory emphasized how markets could run by themselves, seemingly without the need for explicit design. The eighteenth-century Scottish philosopher and economist Adam Smith famously described how the "invisible hand" of the market refuted his contemporaries' concerns that, with the decline of feudalism, the absence of anyone to control production would lead to economic chaos. The reason he gave was that if any goods were in short supply, prices for those goods would rise to promote increased production and to encourage reduced usage, and similarly, surpluses would lead producers to cut back—all as if guided by an invisible hand.

A more modern account highlights the assumptions that would be required for various of Smith's conclusions to be justified. Kenneth Arrow and Gerard Debreu famously formulated a model that addresses the conclusion that prices can guide the economy to an efficient outcome and includes the assumption known as *perfect competition*. A market is competitive to the extent that whenever one party to a transaction demands significantly more favorable terms than the prevailing ones, there are other suppliers or customers who are willing to replace that party and participate in the same transaction according to the prevailing terms. In a perfectly competitive economy, each individual participant, acting alone, has zero influence on the terms of trade. The economic system with all its participants, balancing supply and demand, determines those terms. Adding other assumptions, including that each household cares only about its own consumption and is never satiated, always wanting more of at least some goods, leads to the first welfare theorem: in a perfectly competitive economy, if the prevailing prices are such that the supply is equal to the demand for every type of good, then *there is no other feasible allocation that makes one agent better off without making another worse off.* An allocation with the italicized property is said to be *Pareto efficient*, in honor of the famous economist Vilfredo Pareto, who introduced this criterion.

Like the Coase theorem, the first welfare theorem relies on assumptions that in some real situations fail to hold even approximately. For example, the mathematical model used to prove the theorem assumes that each market participant affects others only by trading with them. When one person's or company's consumption or production decision directly affects another person's welfare or another company's ability to produce, that is called an "externality." Externalities are common and can be *negative* or *positive*. For example, a homeowner may use her noisy lawnmower too early in the morning, disturbing her neighbors' ability to sleep. This is a negative externality, because the neighbors' welfare is harmed by the homeowner's choice. An example of a *positive* externality is the consequence of Apple's development and marketing of its iPhone. That decision spawned valuable new opportunities for app developers, whose products were complementary to Apple's. Like many new products, by making consumers aware and by proving that consumers would demand this product, the iPhone also created new market opportunities for competing products like Google's Android operating system and the smartphones produced by Samsung, Lenovo, and HTC. According to the neoclassical theory, markets do not sufficiently deter activities with negative externalities nor do they sufficiently reward activities with positive externalities. Many of the rules of social interaction in markets and other settings are designed to mitigate or eliminate negative externalities. For example, rules that prevent drivers of cars from blocking an intersection can enable other drivers to reach their destinations more quickly and safely.

Externalities are not the only real-world complication that upsets the conclusion of the first welfare theorem. Its foundational assumption is that markets are perfectly competitive, but some are far from it, because some participants have substantial power to set or affect prices. Apple, for example, had considerable flexibility in pricing the iPhone: its high price relative to the products of its competitors cost it some sales, but the sales it did make were much more profitable.

These first two reasons for failures of unorganized markets—externalities and imperfect competition—are discussed at length in all elementary microeconomics textbooks. But there are two more assumptions that receive much less discussion in textbooks but are of critical importance for market design. The first is the assumption that consumers and firms do not care which units they may receive or supply of each product and consequently that the only relevant constraints on market transactions are that the quantity demanded must be equal to the quantity supplied. The second is that prices exist at which supply is equal to demand. The Arrow-Debreu model incorporates the first of these assumptions. A theorem about that model identifies mathematical conditions, related to the convexity of certain sets, that are sufficient to imply the second—that market-clearing prices exist.

Why does the Arrow-Debreu model, like most other economic models, assume that products in a category are homogeneous? The traditional answer is that if two items are different in any important way, whether that be physical characteristics or their time and place of availability, then they can just be treated as different products with different prices. A traveler who needs a hotel room in New York City on Tuesday is not likely to be satisfied by a room in a different city or in the same city on a different day, so rooms in different cities or on different days are different products and can have different prices. The trouble with this answer is that it can be carried only so far. There can be only one physical product at any exact location and time. If product descriptions must respect every distinction, then every supplier of any physical product is a monopolist and every unit of every item has its own price! These are troubling conclusions for a model of an economy based on competition or in which individual choices are supposed to be guided by the knowledge of every price of every product.

In reality, some details of time and place and even physical characteristics are always overlooked in defining a product category. As a consequence, some heterogeneity always remains. For example, although nonexperts may think of bushels of wheat as homogeneous, the physical characteristics defining "number 2 red wheat" include limits on the minimum weight per bushel of wheat, the maximum fraction of damaged kernels, the percentage of white wheat kernels mixed in with the red wheat kernels, the amount of foreign material, and so on.[1] The commodity "number 2 red winter wheat in Chicago" is defined by a range of times and places that the wheat will be available, in addition to the range of physical characteristics just described.

In some applications, very fine differences among products within a category are critically important for serving demand. The electricity market may be organized to pay generators the same price for electric power delivered at 5:00 p.m. and 5:04 p.m., but a user who flips a switch at 5:00 p.m. cannot use the power available at 5:04 p.m. The electricity system needs to be managed to deliver what users demand when they demand it, and not just a certain total number of megawatts at a particular location in the time interval from 5:00 to 5:05 p.m.

Resource constraints—for example, the statement that the supply of electricity is sufficient to meet demand—differ among markets in qualitatively important ways. I will call a resource constraint "simple" if, when people attempt to violate it, the only consequence is that some demand is left unserved. For example, if three people show up to drive two cars at a car rental company, one of them will be disappointed. Traditional economic analyses, which extoll the ability of price adjustments to correct imbalances of demand and supply, implicitly assume that all constraints are simple. However, for some resource constraints, attempted violations can have less benign consequences. For example, if two trains try to use the same segment of track at the same time, the consequence is not merely that one finds the track unavailable: they risk a disastrous collision. Adam Smith's account of prices eventually adjusting so that resources are not continually over-demanded is poor consolation for the riders on those trains! When even temporary imbalances of supply and demand are intolerable, a system of prices alone is just not good enough: some other means of coordination is needed to ensure no imbalance. Another example is drawn from electricity markets. When the demand for electrical power exceeds the capacity of the electricity transmission network, there can be brownouts or blackouts that affect all consumers.

In this monograph, I recognize two kinds of complexity that often interact to make centralization of markets desirable and good market design valuable. First, when the plans of many individuals need to satisfy constraints to avoid incurring the very high costs associated with such events as train crashes and brownouts, the constraint is not simple. Second, when heterogeneity within a product category implies that acceptable market performance may require producing and assigning the right units of products to individual users, I refer to those acceptability constraints as complex as well. The two sources of complexity are often found together. When they are present, the classical economic conception—in which individual adjustments in firms' and consumers' decisions, guided by prices, resolves temporary conditions of excess supply or demand—is not a suitable basis for a theory of market design.[2]

The second underappreciated assumption that I have highlighted is that market-clearing prices must exist. Arrow and Debreu have proven in their model that if certain sets are convex, then market-clearing prices exist. But their convex-sets assumptions are not innocuous. Among the implications of those assumptions are that all goods can be made and used, not only in whole units but in fractional units as well, and that production processes can be scaled up or down without losing efficiency. In reality, there are some goods like sugar and wheat and paint that can be consumed in fractional units, but goods like houses are consumed only in integer quantities. Persian rugs can evidently be made as effectively at small or large scales, but some manufacturing processes, like auto assembly, are far more efficient when done at large scales. In such cases, the convexity assumptions apply poorly, and prices may need to be supplemented with other market data to inform and guide manufacturing decisions.

Issues of complexity are rarely addressed in economic discourse, and that blindness probably explains much of the resistance to the ideas of market design. Without complexity, what contribution could a market designer possibly make? According to the dogma that comes from a too literal reading of the Coase theorem, people should always be left to arrange their own trades, because they know their own preferences best. Those who take the competitive model and its associated first welfare theorem too literally are also tempted to ignore the problems of complex constraints, instead concluding with Adam Smith that, so long as markets are reasonably competitive, the invisible hand of unregulated competition will guide the participants to an efficient outcome.

One school of thought based on this tradition teaches students to recognize particular situations in which a well-motivated regulator, with enough information and policy tools at its disposal, could improve on ordinary market outcomes. Market regulations might perhaps be justified to discourage activities with negative externalities or to encourage activities with positive externalities. Regulation might be justified to curb market power, for example, preventing monopolists from manipulating prices in damaging ways. In reality, however, perfect regulation is not possible: regulations require the creation of regulatory bureaucracies with rigid missions of their own, often leading to excessive and/or counterproductive regulations. Generally, the theory of competitive markets tends to work in parallel with the Coasian analysis to reaffirm the idea that competitive markets mostly take care of themselves well enough to make it proper to avoid the cost of regulatory bureaucracy. In this view, so long as the parties can bargain reasonably freely to reach mutually beneficial agreements, and particularly when competition disciplines those who would manipulate prices, unregulated markets can operate much more efficiently than a market governed by a regulator, who may be too corrupt or too ill-informed to do anything of real value. Many economists who subscribe to these traditional perspectives argue that market transactions are best left to the parties involved, without any attempt at external organization or intervention.

The novel perspective in this book is that complexity can, by itself, provide an important reason why some markets benefit from careful organization. To make that point, before launching into the formalities, let me investigate the ways complexity can and sometimes has caused unregulated, decentralized markets to fail and how, in such cases, details of market design can affect market performance.

1.1 LAND ALLOCATION IN GEORGIA

One indisputable premise of the traditional view is that any inefficient resource allocation creates an incentive for parties to straighten out this problem to create value in which they might all share. However, when the relevant constraints are more complex than simply deciding who gets how much of a limited resource, the parties can benefit from some formal organization: it can be difficult for them to find an efficient allocation on their own without a careful market organization.

Consider a study of land allocation in Georgia conducted by Hoyt Bleakley and Joseph Ferrie (2014). Between 1803 and 1832, Georgia opened land on its frontier using a series of land lotteries (figure 1.1).

In each lottery, applicants drew pieces of paper from a barrel to determine which plot of land each applicant would receive (figure 1.2).

The plots were sized with small farms in mind, reflecting the farming technology of the time. However, many of the lottery winners did not initially move to the land to develop their plots, and by the time they did, the technology had changed to favor larger farms. Could the market reorganize ownership without assistance, with owners making the necessary transactions to assemble efficiently sized plots for farming?

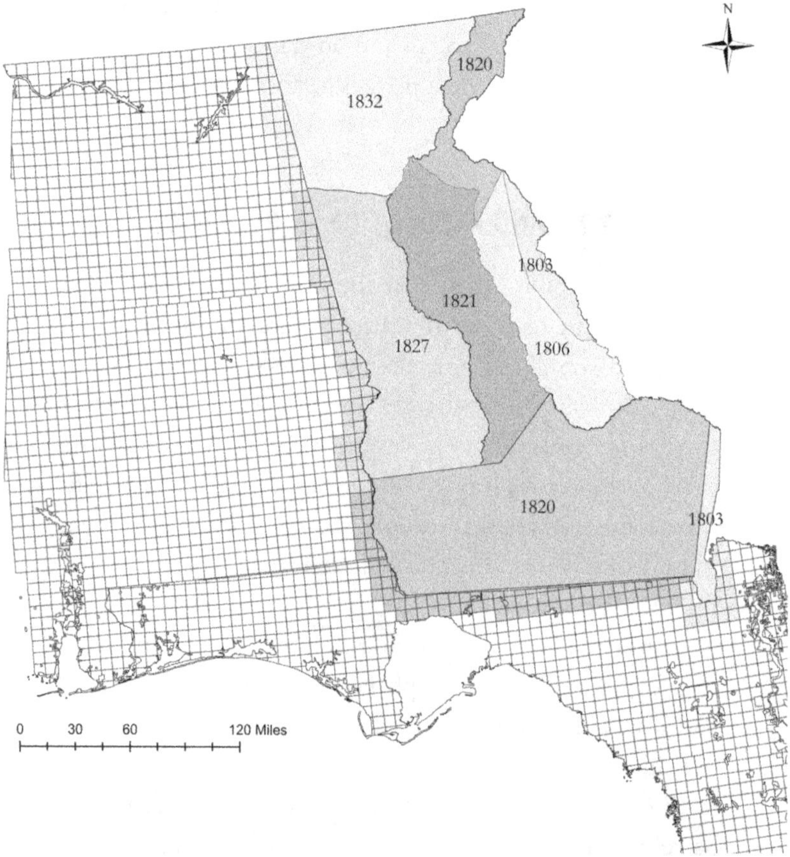

Figure 1.1 Georgia land-lottery areas and years. Figure from Bleakley and Ferrie (2014).

Such a reorganization of ownership is challenging, because it involves more than just deciding how much land should be allocated to each owner. To illustrate the complexity, imagine that the initial allocation of plots and the desired

Figure 1.2 Lottery participants drawing plot numbers from barrels. Artwork by George I. Parrish Jr.

allocation are as shown in figure 1.3. The dashed rectangles in the figure outline an initial land allocation with small plots, while the solid rectangles illustrate the larger plots required for efficient allocation.

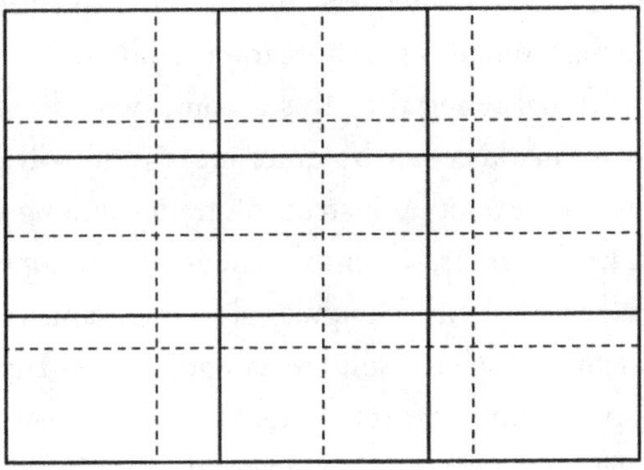

Figure 1.3 Achieving fully efficient land use can require complex changes in lot structure and ownership.

Each of the solid rectangles intersects four dashed rectangles. If all of the trades needed for efficiency were to be made individually, then each of the nine owners of a new solid rectangular plot must make a deal with four owners of dashed rectangular plots, which would require thirty-six deals in all. For twelve of the dashed rectangle owners (excluding the ones in the four corners), their first deals would break up their lots, leaving the seller with a smaller, less efficient, and oddly shaped plot. For the first deal to be profitable, a dashed rectangle owner may have to anticipate that he will make several other related deals later, at a time when his diminished lot may have already weakened his bargaining position.

The sheer number of transactions required challenges Coasian reasoning. For while it is true that an inefficient arrangement of rights provides an incentive for trade, when very many trades are required, unorganized and unregulated trading may take a long time to work out the problem, particularly when some of the required trades require the owners to accept even smaller, less efficient plots, in anticipation that they may someday sell those for a profit.

A traditional rebuttal to this account would emphasize that private markets can be quite creative in solving such problems. For example, instead of trades among the initial and final owners, an entrepreneur or developer could acquire all the dashed rectangular plots, reorganize and subdivide them, and sell the solid rectangular parts. That would involve sixteen purchase transactions and nine sales transactions, twenty-five transactions in total. That is still a large number, though less than the thirty-six of the first option, and it frees the owners of the small rectangles from having to

Figure 1.4 Shopping mall in Seattle with holdout home ("nail house"). Photo courtesy of Geoff Carter.

deal with multiple buyers. This is better, but it is no panacea. Some of the small-plot owners who could block the efficient assignment might demand a particularly high price, making the development barely profitable.

Holdouts of this sort are a common problem in land transactions. Homes that land redevelopers are unable to buy and eventually have to build around are sometimes called "nail houses," because while construction goes on around them, they stand out like nails that need to be pounded down.[3] Figure 1.4 shows a Seattle shopping mall that was built around a home whose owner held out too long, demanding a too-high price.

Owners of other kinds of buildings besides private homes have also been known to hold out, leading to oddly structured developments. Saint Joseph's Catholic Church in San Antonio, Texas, shown in figure 1.5 with its surrounding development, is one such case.

These examples illustrate that even when the stakes are high, getting the unanimous approval of property owners for

Figure 1.5 Saint Joseph's Catholic Church and its surrounding development. Photo from Wikipedia.

a new development can be challenging. As the photographs emphasize, such failures can lead to costly and long-lived oddities with which nobody is completely satisfied.

The nail-house and church cases, however interesting they may be, are just anecdotes. Is this actually a common and important problem in land reallocation?

The Georgia land holdings example helps to illuminate the issue more generally, because it involves a sufficiently large number of similar plots of land to allow the application of statistical methods. Bleakley and Ferrie take advantage of the fact that the initial landownership was determined randomly, which created some inconvenient ownership patterns, and that technical change meant that larger plots would become more efficient for farming. They use the changes to study how long it takes for unorganized trading among individuals to unwind inefficiencies and find that most plots of land remained in the hands of their original owners or the owners' direct descendants for a very long time: about one hundred years! The same study also showed that this slow reallocation meant substantial losses for the landowners. Prices of land in Georgia were about 20 percent lower than similar, adjacent farmland in Florida, which the authors attribute to the smaller plots and consequent lower productivity of that land. Such a loss of value provided incentives to make private trades, but without the right support for the market, such incentives were not enough. One factor that helped break the logjam of failed transactions was a shift to better ownership records, which helped buyers and sellers locate one another. Eventually, ownership patterns changed, and larger, more efficient plots became the norm. The century-long delay in making this transition, however, wasted a tremendous amount of economic value. That was the direct consequence of the complexity of the required transactions and the absence of good, centralized property records to make efficient trade possible.

This story of changing landownership overstates the difficulty of improving efficiency in some ways but understates it in others. The case is overstated because, depending on the details of the scale economies, a buyer might achieve a fairly efficient outcome merely by assembling two adjacent lots into a double-sized lot rather than one of the optimal intermediate size. That is a much easier transaction to arrange, and such fallback arrangements also reduce the power of an individual owner to block efficient reorganization by holding out. The nail-house cases illustrate the positive side of that point, showing that a project can still be completed if there is a single holdout. But they also illustrate an important negative point, namely, that a failure to get the allocation right when the reorganization is happening can lead to an inefficient development that is nearly permanent. For even if the owner of the Seattle nail house would now like to sell, the developer is unlikely to be interested: the development was redesigned and built to omit that plot. It is too late to undo the damage and inefficiency from the initial failure to trade.

It is precisely the sort of difficulty depicted in these examples that motivates the law surrounding *eminent domain*, which allows governments to seize property in exchange for reasonable compensation to promote public projects. While the scope of this governmental right remains controversial, some uses seem obvious. During the building of the interstate highways in the United States, for example, individual property owners were prevented from holding up projects by refusing attempts to purchase land at prices determined to be the land's "fair market value."

These cases teach several important lessons about how markets work and why organization may matter. First and most obviously, unorganized markets can take a very long time to correct any misallocation, particularly when the transactions are complex and require a multilateral reorganization within a heterogeneous product category such as land. Second, opportunities to create value—by designing a more logical development, for example—can be irretrievably lost when some parties are excluded from the initial deal. Third, the details of how a market is organized and operates can affect the efficiency of exchange. In the early period of the Georgia land case, efficient reorganization of ownership was thwarted by the sheer difficulty that potential buyers had in finding and communicating with the owners who might sell the land. As land records improved to include the contact information of the owners, trade became easier.[4] Fourth, the details of property rights can affect the ease of assembling and repackaging land holdings. We illustrated this in connection with the government's use of eminent domain, which contributed importantly in redeveloping urban areas, building the U.S. national highway network, and more.

1.2 AIRLINE ROUTES AND COMMERCIAL SPACE LAUNCHES

Some allocation problems seem so complex that people rarely consider using markets to govern them. An example is the allocation of airline routes or of takeoff and landing slots at major, congested airports. For airline flights to be safe, adequate time and space between flights are needed, both in the air and during takeoffs and landings. Safety requirements change in the short and long term; for instance, changes in weather affect the safe spacing of planes during takeoff and landing, while new technologies, such as commercial drones, raise new issues about how to share the airspace. These considerations make a completely decentralized, unorganized market dangerous and have prompted the development of a system governed by route planners and air traffic controllers.

But centralized systems suffer disadvantages too, and something important is lost when prices are removed from their role in guiding allocations. When users need to pay a price to use a resource, they are encouraged to economize on it. A commercial airline might economize by scheduling fewer flights carrying more passengers or might divert flights to a nearby airport with less-congested runways. A package service might schedule its flights at night, when there is less passenger traffic. Drone flights might fly at lower altitudes, where schedules might be more fluid. And as uses and needs change, new users with more valuable applications can buy property rights from existing users to ease the transition. In a full free market system, the pattern of investment is even deeper. Aircraft companies design and build planes to service the most valuable uses. As costs rise on expensive routes, retail prices of flying on the most congested routes may also rise, and some consumers may switch to trains or buses. As the theory of competitive markets emphasizes, the prices that emerge from competition provide the right incentives throughout the system for travelers, airlines, aircraft manufacturers, and other travel suppliers to make the correct choices to use resources efficiently.

Lifting our eyes to the skies, we see another new use of airspace peeking over the horizon. Over the past few years in the United States and Europe, there has been growing interest in the promise of commercial space launches, challenging air traffic control systems to coordinate the new vertical flights with traditional horizontal ones. The smart allocation of airspace between these requires using information about their relative values—something that markets almost always determine better than regulators can.

We know from precedent that commercial space launches can be disruptive: U.S. government space launches from Cape Canaveral in Florida have led to major disruptions, forcing changes in flight routes along the whole Eastern Seaboard of the United States. This is because the accident rate for space launches is much higher than for commercial aircraft and also because accidents involving space launches can fling debris over a radius of hundreds of miles.

On October 31, 2014, just weeks before I gave the Arrow lecture on which this book is based, Virgin Galactic's VSS *Enterprise* crashed in California's Mojave Desert. The crash, pictured in figure 1.6, spread debris over thirty-four miles

Figure 1.6 Virgin Galactic's VSS *Enterprise*, before and after. Top photo by Jurvetson on Flickr; bottom photo by National Transportation Safety Board.

of desert, highlighting the importance of providing extra time and space around vertical flights, relative to horizontal ones.

These facts raise several resource-allocation issues. Which vertical flights should be scheduled at all? At what times and from which locations? Should some vertical flights be scheduled at night, when horizontal traffic is less dense and time sensitive? Should they be scheduled only at some distance from major air routes or airports? Which characteristics of space launches should determine their priorities and standing against horizontal flights?

Systems based on pricing are helpful for answering questions like these. If a vertical flight—a space launch—displaces many valuable horizontal flights that own the rights to their routings, a market system would force the launch to buy those rights. Or, if the rights were controlled and sold by the government, a market system would require the launch to outbid the horizontal flights. Launches that were not worthwhile would be discouraged, and if a launch could be conveniently rescheduled to displace fewer or less valuable horizontal flights, the price system would encourage people to make such adjustments.

A system based on governmental regulation alone normally lacks such good incentives. Shown in figure 1.7 is an artist's rendering of the planned Front Range Spaceport, which is to be built six miles west of Denver airport.

One may wonder whether this location, so close to a major airline hub for the western United States, is a good one, or whether such a choice adds needlessly to air traffic

Figure 1.7 Artist's rendering of the planned Front Range Spaceport. Luis Vidal+Architects.

congestion. Without prices on air routes and takeoff and landing slots for different seasons and different times of day, it is hard for anyone, including the planners, to assess the wisdom of this choice.

As this example shows, even in a tightly constrained system, there can be an important role for prices in guiding resource allocation: to encourage individual agents in the market to take account of the opportunity costs of the resources that they use. It would be foolish, however, to conclude that it is best to rely on an unregulated market, without a central authority to monitor safety constraints. The challenge is to incorporate prices in an effective way while still maintaining enough direct control to ensure that complex constraints are satisfied.

1.3 THE FCC'S INCENTIVE AUCTION

The lessons of the first two examples were applied in 2016 in the ambitious "incentive auction" conducted by the U.S. Federal Communications Commission (FCC). Through my company Auctionomics, I led the consulting team that designed, planned, and created specialized software for this auction, so I will discuss the context and details for this example in more detail than the previous two. (I also include a detailed description of the main auction rules at the end of this chapter.)

Like the Georgia land example, the FCC's incentive auction is about reallocating property rights to achieve more efficient use of a valuable resource. In the FCC case, the rights to be reallocated are not those to use plots of land but rather to use frequencies of radio spectrum. Before describing the challenges to such a reallocation, let us first review the historical uses of this spectrum and how recent changes in technology led to changing patterns of demand that make such a reallocation extremely valuable.

Cable television was first introduced in the United States in 1948, but in its early years it was simply a complement to over-the-air broadcast television, allowing stations to reach viewers outside their broadcast areas. The cable company would receive broadcast signals on its own antenna and retransmit them along a wire to individual households. Most viewers still received their local stations over the air, but some viewers supplemented those with additional stations that they could receive only over cable. At first, the increased range of larger stations merely created competition among local stations in nearby communities, but as time passed, the broadcast model evolved. In 1976 the first cable network station not based in any local area (Ted Turner's superstation WTCG) began operation. As more viewers came to use cable and more stations became available on the system, consumers relied less on the rooftop antennas and "rabbit ears" on top of their televisions, even for local programming. Satellite television companies entered the market to compete with cable companies. By 2012 some 90 percent of U.S. households had a TV signal from cable or satellite, greatly reducing the number of viewers relying solely on over-the-air broadcasts. Meanwhile, a second force was at work that also reduced television broadcasters' demand for spectrum: the development of digital television technology. The new technology made it possible for broadcasters to send high-definition TV signals to households using only a fraction of the 6 MHz bandwidth that had initially been set aside for the older, analog standard-definition signals. The excess bandwidth has been used mainly to broadcast additional stations that are watched by few viewers, so much of this spectrum could be reassigned to other uses with only a modest loss of economic value.

Even as the value of over-the-air TV broadcasting has declined, new uses for that spectrum have emerged. The introduction of the Apple iPhone in 2007 proved to be a watershed, initiating explosive growth in the demand for wireless Internet services, which soon led to a shortage of radio spectrum suitable for carrying wireless data. In the United States in 2012, the White House announced a goal of clearing 500 MHz of bandwidth—a vast amount of spectrum—for wireless Internet by reallocating it from other uses.

Over-the-air television broadcasting has used two different ranges of frequencies, known as VHF (very high frequency), which originally corresponded to TV channels 2–13, and UHF (ultra-high frequency), which was originally used for channels 14 and higher.[5] The UHF broadcast channels use much higher frequencies than VHF, and in the old days of analog broadcasting, it was the VHF channels that were more valuable. Today, it is the UHF frequencies, especially those between 600 and 700 MHz, that are particularly valuable for transmitting wireless data to mobile devices. Signals on lower frequencies propagate better than ones on higher frequencies, covering longer distances and passing more easily through such obstacles as trees, raindrops, and the thick walls of urban office towers. Much lower frequencies are less suitable for mobile data, both because they require larger antennas that are not easily fit into mobile devices and because very low frequencies may encounter interference from devices like vacuum cleaners and kitchen blenders. For providing wide area coverage, the 600–700 MHz band is the most valuable "beachfront property" among the available wireless bands.

Just as in the land-reallocation example discussed earlier, radio-spectrum reallocation requires subdividing and repackaging old property packages to create ones that are more suitable for the new technology. In the discussion of land allocation, I focused on a simple conceptual model in which buyers care only about the land that they own, but the reality is more complex than that. Owners of residential lots may care that their neighbors' music is not too loud, that the nearby theater and clubs provide adequate parking to avoid overflow and attract law-abiding patrons, that the community parks are suitable for the number of residents, and so on. The owners of those nail houses care not only about owning and using their own lots but also about the structures and activity on nearby lots.

Similar issues involving "good neighbors" arise in radio-spectrum allocation. One example is the case of a mobile phone that is operating just a few feet from a television set that is receiving an over-the-air TV signal. Just as a human adjusts the volume of his voice so that a listener can hear his speech, the phone handset adjusts the power of the signal it transmits to reach its cell tower, turning the power up when the tower is more distant. As for the TV, if the set is far from the TV broadcast tower, then it receives only a weak signal. When the phone handset sends a powerful signal, the TV faces a challenge, much like that of a human trying to listen to a voice from a long way across the room when a neighbor is playing loud music: the loud telephone signal can make it impossible for the TV set to "hear" the TV broadcast signal. Interference can also happen in a reverse way, with a loud TV signal drowning out a telephone signal on a nearby frequency, making it impossible for the phone to "hear" the message sent to it by the cell tower. The engineering solution to this problem is to arrange the allocation so that TV and phone signals are never using adjacent frequencies. Doing that requires putting all the TV signals into one set of adjacent frequencies, the mobile signals into another set, and leaving a third set of frequencies (mostly) unused to serve as a "guard band" between the TV and mobile uses.

A related challenge is that downlink signals (which travel from the cell tower to the phone or other device) can interfere with uplink signals (which travel from the device to the cell tower). If the phone is far from the tower, then the downlink signal may be weak and a phone's own uplink, which needs to be loud to reach the tower, can drown out a downlink on an adjacent frequency. The solution to this problem in North America and Europe is to use separate frequencies for uplink and downlink with a guard band—frequencies that are not used for uplink or downlink or any potentially conflicting service.

This organization of radio frequencies for different uses, with guard bands in between, is reminiscent of good land use policy, with commercial, industrial, and residential sectors and with alleys or parks and rural areas often serving as buffers between the different uses. Just as land use can be hard to change once fixed structures have been built, spectrum use can be hard to change once consumer devices like phone handsets and television sets have been widely distributed with their radios tuned to operate on particular frequencies and TV broadcast stations and cell sites have been located and provisioned to use particular frequencies. Further complicating the problem of change is that for mobile devices to be useful nationally and even internationally, the same frequencies must be devoted to mobile communications in different geographic areas.

Even more than in our land example, these characteristics of radio-spectrum engineering make it critically important to coordinate uses over a wide set of potential buyers and sellers. If a TV broadcaster using channel 41 in New York is to be shut down or moved to make room for a wireless mobile service, then for spectrum to be used efficiently, broadcasters on channel 41 in Topeka and San Diego and other cities across the country must also be shut down or moved, and at roughly the same time. And if channel 41 is in the middle of a contiguous set of channels that will be used for wireless service, then compatible changes need to be made on channels 40 and 42 at the same time. Moreover, to standardize licenses and make them largely interchangeable, the "band plan" calls for a fixed separation of frequencies, such as 40 MHz, between the uplink and downlink frequencies of any license. This, too, requires coordination in uses between distant frequencies. Finally, guard bands, which are not used directly by any of the services but are necessary to enable them all, need to be provided by somebody, and the cost of that needs to be suitably shared.

That television stations cannot legally be required to give up their broadcast rights creates yet another layer of difficulty. What frequencies (channels) are to be assigned to TV broadcasters that choose *not* to sell and instead continue to broadcast? Answering that question inspired several of the most important innovations in market design for the FCC broadcast incentive auction.

The problem of assigning channels to broadcasters is particularly difficult given that TV broadcast signals from one station can be detected by the antenna of a household that may be two hundred miles away. So two stations as far as four hundred miles apart can potentially interfere with one another's signals. Thus the assignment of frequencies to broadcasters in, say, New York City constrains the assignments in Connecticut and New Jersey, which in turn constrain the assignments in neighboring cities, and eventually throughout the entire continental United States, and even Canada and Mexico.

This complex interaction is depicted in figure 1.8. The figure shows a map of the United States and Canada and includes a node to represent each TV location. An arc connects two nodes if the two stations cannot both be assigned to the same channel (usually because they are too close geographically). The web of arcs shows that nearly all stations in the United States and Canada are connected at least indirectly through a series of arcs; no station or region can be considered in isolation when deciding channel assignments. Each channel assignment depends on the channels assigned

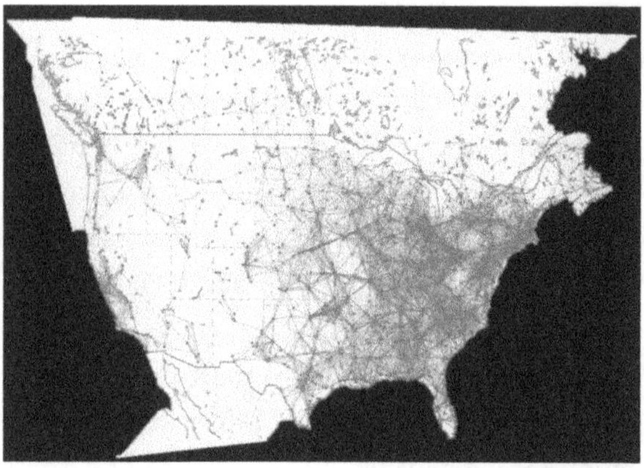

Figure 1.8 Map of cochannel interference links among UHF television stations in the United States.

to its neighboring stations, which in turn depend on the channels assigned to their neighbors, and so on. The interference graph is especially dense east of the Mississippi River, and the assignments in Los Angeles and San Diego are further constrained by treaty requirements to protect Mexican broadcast stations from interferences.

The problem of optimizing the assignment of channels to stations is very hard, even for a fast computer. Indeed, just checking the feasibility of keeping any particular set of stations on air—determining whether there is any way to assign channels to television stations without creating interference—is a difficult computational problem, similar to what mathematicians call a "graph-coloring" problem. This computational difficulty is an important factor influencing the market design, so let us examine the connection between the channel-assignment problem and graph coloring.

In mathematics, a graph is a pair of sets, called "nodes" and "arcs," in which each arc is identified by the pair of nodes that it connects. To understand how this mathematical abstraction applies to the TV channel-assignment problem, let us temporarily imagine that the only constraints on assignments are limits on the set of available channels and a restriction, called the "cochannel constraints," specifying that two stations that are too close to one another physically cannot both be assigned to the same channel.

The actual graph of cochannel constraints for the U.S. incentive auction is depicted in figure 1.8, superimposed on an outline of the mainland United States and part of Canada. Each dot in the figure represents a television broadcast station, which is a "node" in the graph. Each line segment is an "arc" representing a pair of stations that cannot be assigned to the same TV channel without creating unacceptable broadcast interference. The mathematical graph-coloring problem asks this question: Given a finite set of colors (here colors represent TV channels such as channel 18 or channel 30), is it possible to assign a color to each node so that no pair of nodes connected by an arc are the same color? Graph coloring gives an exact account of the channel-assignment problem with only cochannel constraints, although the real problem has some additional constraints that we will not explore in any detail in this book.[6] Thus, the actual problem has a more complex structure than its associated graph-coloring problem.

What makes this graph-coloring characterization important is a result in a branch of computer science known as complexity theory, which characterizes the hardness of certain kinds of computations. Graph-coloring problems are computationally very hard, even in theory. Newcomers to computing theory, impressed by the version of Moore's law predicting that processors will continue to double in speed every two years, may imagine that all computational problems that are not yet easy for computers will soon become so. We just need to wait awhile, they may think, as computers grow faster. What the newcomers' view fails to reckon with is just how hard some ordinary-looking computational problems can be and how fast the difficulty grows with the size of the problem. For example, suppose we have a graph-coloring problem with $C = 10$ colors, N nodes, and A arcs, and we want to know whether there is any way to color the nodes that satisfies all the constraints. There are ten ways to assign a color to the first node and, for each of those, ten ways to assign colors to the second node, and so on. So, there 10^N different combinations of ways to assign colors to nodes. Suppose that in 1965, when Moore first stated his law, it would have been possible with a day of computing time to solve this graph-coloring problem with $N = 200$ nodes. Half a century later, if computer speeds have doubled every two years, then modern computers are more than 33,000,000 times faster than they were in 1965—a huge improvement. But for graph coloring, it means only that with a day of computing time, it is now possible to solve problems with $N = 207$ or perhaps $N = 208$, because those sizes present 10,000,000 times and 100,000,000 times more possible combinations to be checked. In the actual problem, N is about 2,400, so even if Moore's law continued to apply, it would take more than 40,000 years of additional improvements before a computer would be fast enough to check all the possibilities in this application in a single day.

A reader might point out an assumption of the preceding analysis, namely, that I have assumed that each node needs to be checked separately. Some kinds of large computational problems, the reader might rightly say, are actually very easy: they can be solved quickly by using a smart algorithm that skips over most of the irrelevant possibilities and homes in directly on just a small subset of interesting alternatives. How do we know that there is no such algorithm for graph-coloring problems?

The answer to that question depends on a deep result from complexity theory in computer science. Complexity theory provides a way to distinguish a certain class of easy problems called "P"—for which algorithms exist that are guaranteed to find solutions quickly even for relatively large problems—from the harder classes of so-called "NP-complete" problems, for which there are no such algorithms. The class of graph-coloring problems is NP-complete. It is a standard hypothesis in computer science that "P ≠ NP." If true, that means that for every computational algorithm, there are some problems in any NP-complete class that confound the algorithm, causing its solution times to be very, very long, even relative to the size of the problem.[7] In any case, there are no algorithms that are known to be fast for any class of NP-complete problems, including graph-coloring problems. For all known algorithms, the solution times may grow exponentially with the size of the problem, just as in our Moore's law analysis. The channel-assignment problem is very hard.

The United States and Canada have agreed to coordinate on the spectrum reallocation problem. For the roughly three thousand television stations in those countries, there are about 2.7 million logical constraints that restrict the assignments of TV channels to stations. A typical constraint has one of two forms: either "it is not possible both to assign station A to channel X and to assign station B to channel Y" or "station A must be assigned to exactly one of the channels 14 through Z." Allocating spectrum resources subject to such a large number of constraints exemplifies the challenge in bringing a price-based market solution to complex problems of resource allocation. Neoclassical economic theory ignores the possibility that some optimization problems may be too hard for agents, or even for the fastest computer, but we have seen that radio-spectrum allocations involve just such a problem. It is not hard to imagine how finding the optimal allocation of takeoff and landing slots may also be too hard for even the fastest computers. Studying how prices can be used to guide resource allocation in settings where optimization is effectively impossible is a new research frontier that requires new approaches.

The market design developed to overcome these challenges involved several elements that have already been discussed. First, in 2012 Congress clarified the ambiguous rights of TV broadcasters to use frequencies for over-the-air broadcasting. It held that certain types of broadcasters had a right to continue broadcasting with no increase in interference but not necessarily on the same channels they were currently using.[8] To illustrate, suppose that the FCC decided to clear channels 38–51 from TV broadcasting and to use those frequencies instead for mobile wireless services. In such a case, a broadcaster using channel 49 might be required to retune its broadcast to use channel 22 to get out of the way of the new broadband use. The law promised that the government would pay the broadcaster's retuning cost up to a total amount specified in the statute and that it would make "all reasonable efforts" to ensure that the station could reach the same set of viewers after retuning as it had before.

This specification of broadcasters' rights was a crucial detail for operating a successful market. It is analogous in some ways to the right of a landowner whose property is subject to eminent domain. In this case, the analogue of fair compensation is a different broadcast channel and cash compensation for the costs of retuning the transmission equipment to use the new channel.

To highlight the importance of this detail, suppose that broadcasters instead had the right to continue broadcasting on the same particular channels. In that hypothetical case, if efficient spectrum reorganization requires that channels 38–51 be cleared of all broadcast activity, then every individual broadcaster using one of those channels in every city nationwide would have the ability to derail the reassignment. This would likely either make the transition prohibitively expensive or result in the equivalent of "spectrum nail houses"—stations broadcasting in frequencies that are surrounded, geographically and in terms of frequencies, by mobile wireless uses. Such spectrum nail houses would create intractable engineering issues, entailing a huge waste of value.

The inherent complexity of this resource allocation poses another important challenge for market design, namely, that excessive complexity of market rules can discourage people from participating. Even with the clear and helpful property rights that Congress established, owners of TV stations are likely to find any market design in this context to have elements that are confusing. When a broadcaster must determine the amount it should bid in an auction to sell its station, few (if any) are likely to understand precisely how the auctioneer will decide which offers to accept. The government's value of any one station depends on all the other stations' offers, but not only on that. It also depends on a complex, opaque computation that is very hard even for fast computers and that station owners might be unable to verify, let alone understand, even after the market has closed. Given such an imperfect understanding, how much should a station owner demand for its station in any negotiation?

A station's inability to make this computation is important, because in a competitive market for TV spectrum, the value of any single station to the owner who is willing to sell should be just a bit lower than the selling price, and the value to the owner who is unwilling to sell should be just a bit higher. This implies that, in a competitive market, the prices offered for broadcast rights after the auction should be close to the auction price. For a station owner who is unsure what price to demand, demanding a high price or just sitting out the auction would then be viable options. If the government hopes that most broadcasters will participate and not demand very high prices, so that there is a chance to clear a lot of spectrum, then it needs to encourage station owners by making it easy for them to participate confidently in the auction. Later, we will see that among the most important innovations in the incentive auction is its solution to this design challenge.

There are also other new challenges that distinguish the incentive auction from earlier radio-spectrum auctions. In previous auctions, the number of licenses for sale has always been fixed in advance, based on the amount of spectrum that the government seller was able to make available. In contrast, for the incentive auction, the total transaction volume depends on bids by both sellers and buyers; that is, on supply and demand. In FCC parlance, auctions in which the FCC sells licenses to new users are called "forward auctions" and auctions in which it acquires licenses from existing users are called "reverse auctions." We will see later that prices quoted during a forward auction are increasing, just as in auctions on a site like eBay or in a live auction house. Prices quoted during a reverse auction are decreasing, as bidders compete by reducing the prices that they demand.

In the incentive auction, the clearing quantity depends on the demand for mobile broadband licenses in a forward auction from mobile phone and data companies and the supply of TV station licenses offered by stations in a reverse auction. In textbook markets, the market-clearing prices and quantities are found by crossing the supply and demand curves to find a price at which the quantity that buyers want to buy is the same as the quantity that sellers want to sell. In the incentive auction, however, things are not so easy as that.

The first problem is computing the supply curve. When a TV station sells its broadcast rights, that does not, by itself, create any usable license for mobile broadband. The number of broadband rights that can be created is the result of a complex computation, with inputs that include the whole set of stations with rights to be purchased. Even determining the feasibility of clearing a set of channels using a particular set of bids is an NP-complete problem, and therefore computationally challenging. Finding the supply curve requires even more; it requires determining the minimum cost of clearing sufficiently many stations to create a set of broadband licenses.

Computing the demand curve is simpler than computing the supply curve but still more difficult than the usual textbook implies. Here, the problem is that there is not just one price for the new broadband licenses but different prices for licenses in different geographic areas, including licenses covering the downtowns of major cities and others covering the suburbs and still others for rural areas. To clear the same TV channels nationwide, the same number of licenses must be sold in each area, and each of those will generate a different price. The sum of those prices represents the total offer by buyers (the "demand price") for any particular amount of spectrum that may be sold. That price needs to be sufficient to pay for all the broadcast rights that must be acquired, and the cost of retuning stations, and certain other costs of the system.

Among our several examples, the incentive auction application is the most complicated one. It combines the need for many coordinated trades of different sorts of goods, the need to make other auxiliary decisions about new TV channel assignments, the importance of introducing prices to guide decisions, a thoughtful assignment of property rights so that a single station in one part of the country is protected but not conferred the power to block a valuable reallocation, a computational problem of daunting complexity, and more.

One last question that is of great interest to many economists is: Why is this a problem for the government? Why not just give the broadcasters the same rights that described earlier and use an auction to sell to a "spectrum property developer" the sole right to reallocate spectrum, including requiring that broadcasters move to new channels? After all, redevelopment agencies that seek to reorganize landholdings in old cities often have a large role for private parties. Is there any compelling reason why it is better to use a government agency than a private party for a spectrum-coordination problem such as this one?

Perhaps the single most compelling advantage to having a government agency conduct the incentive auction is that there are so many legal issues and political decisions involved in the process. What does it mean to make "all reasonable efforts" to preserve the coverage of broadcasters who must switch to a new channel? If a broadcaster loses, say, 0.5 percent of its audience, is that too much? Is the answer the same if the broadcaster also enjoys some gains by reaching new viewers on the new channel? The answers to these questions affect property rights and the assessment of gains and losses. There are huge advantages of creating a political and administrative process in which stakeholders can offer meaningful inputs and have an opportunity to defend their interests without imposing costly court-ordered delays. The way that spectrum rights are reassigned affects interests besides those of TV broadcasters and wireless operators. Decisions must also be made about the size and location of guard bands, which are used to separate the uplink and downlink frequencies in wireless systems and to separate TV broadcast from wireless uses. These guard bands then become available for low-powered but very valuable, unlicensed applications, like wireless microphones or home WiFi systems. For public policy reasons, it might also be valuable to encourage competition in the mobile broadband industry or to protect certain TV stations (for example, ones serving minority communities). For all of these reasons, a government agency has important advantages over a private coordinator for the radio-spectrum reorganization.

Later I will give a preview of what is to come in the rest of the book—and at the end of the chapter, I include an appendix that explains the overall structure and many of the design details of the 2016 FCC Incentive Auction. It also reports on the initial stages of the auction. The auction was not yet complete when this monograph was sent to press.

1.4 STANDING ON THE SHOULDERS OF GIANTS

The theory of auction market design as developed in this book has its intellectual roots in three strands of research that began in the 1950s and early 1960s. The first of these was initiated by Kenneth Arrow and Leo Hurwicz and concerned the stability of auction-based price systems. That research introduced important ideas about the role of substitute goods into the analysis, and their methods were pushed in new directions by Alexander Kelso and Vincent Crawford in their study of auction-like labor markets. The second important strand was the auction theory research building on original work by William Vickrey, which explored the possibility of providing incentives for auction participants to participate truthfully in a process, so that efficient outcomes could be promoted. Finally, there was a strand initiated by George Dantzig, focusing on approximate solutions to very hard computational problems. All of these strands come together in the account I present in this book. I begin by reviewing those contributions from a specialized perspective to highlight the ideas on which I build, and then show how they can be combined to solve a problem of market design and to point forward to new applications.

The approach in this book is distinctively economic in its focus on the roles of prices, substitutes, and complements in economic systems. Many noneconomists are inclined to think that when some activity is determined to be damaging, it is smart simply to ban it, but that can be very wrong. Activities are not chosen in a vacuum, and a ban on one activity can lead to others being substituted to promote the same objective. It can also lead to complementary activities being dropped. To evaluate a proposed regulation, one needs to look at what the proposed replacements ("substitutes") may be and at what effects there may be on supporting activities ("complements"). For example, concern about the emissions of coal-burning plants might lead to considering a ban on those, but whether such a ban is a good idea may depend on the extent to which the plants will be replaced by cleaner gas-fired plants or some potentially more polluting or dangerous type of plant, or offset by reductions in the use of power. All of these are possible substitutes. Evaluating whether, when, and how to implement such a ban also requires looking at the effect on complements, including the coal-mining industry, the jobs it supports, and the communities that are built around them.

Most of economic theory treats simple models of the economy in which prices alone can guide efficient economic decisions, but that conclusion rarely applies exactly in complex systems. As suggested by the title, a major part of this book is about the scope of price-guided decisions. Can prices work effectively as part of a larger system when there are other complex constraints that make prices alone inadequate or when the relatively loose balance between supply and demand is not sufficient? For example, if we want planes not to crash when flying into an airport, it is surely better to have an air traffic controller tracking flights and guiding the pilots than merely to quote high prices at times when the airspace is likely to be congested!

Even when market prices are not, by themselves, sufficient to guide safe and efficient resource allocation, the key concepts of economic theory—substitutes and complements—are often still useful for analyzing economic systems. For example, in planning terminal and runway capacity for an airport, it makes sense to consider what these may support in terms of the number of passengers per hour, even though such a simplified concept cannot fully describe the complex constraints on the set of flights that an airport can manage. And even though passenger capacity is not a homogeneous commodity, setting prices according to the number of passengers served can still work pretty well to promote efficient use of capacity. Similarly, in radio-spectrum allocations, the radio interference constraints are quite complex, but fitting one more TV broadcast station into a city can often be accomplished by taking out one station in the same city or in a nearby one. Such stations are "approximate substitutes." With that property, despite the enormous complexity of the problem of allocating TV channels to stations, setting prices for each channel or station can be a good guide to finding an approximately efficient solution.

Complements can also be an important part of some analyses. In clearing radio spectrum, stations in different cities tend to be complements, because creating valuable new broadband licenses requires clearing an additional channel nationwide, which in turn often requires buying an additional station in each of several different cities. Markets for complements can be much harder than markets for substitutes and can require greater planning and coordination. Similarly, scheduling a flight out from an airport at some hour requires scheduling a landing at the same airport in an earlier hour (so that a plane is available). Many real constraints exhibit simple complementarities like that. One theme that will emerge later is that it is easier and more effective to find ways to use market-based prices to guide substitution than to do the same for decisions involving complements.

Even when prices to guide efficient resource allocation exist in theory, the practical problem of finding those prices can still be daunting. The information that is needed to set the right price for any resource is typically distributed among the many suppliers and demanders of the resource, and the information for each is privately held. Only the airline knows how much it would lose by moving its landing time in Chicago to a time one hour earlier than its ideal; only the TV broadcaster knows how effectively it could still serve its audience if it gives up its over-the-air channel and instead uses other technologies, including cable and satellite broadcasts, Internet delivery, or a channel-sharing deal with a neighboring station.

The best way to find such prices is often an auction of some kind. This book studies auctions and other bidding-based mechanisms to describe how prices can be discovered and used to guide resource allocation.

As already described, auctions are most effective when goods are substitutes, or nearly so. In the next chapter, we describe the theory of how prices can be determined by auctions when goods are substitutes, building on the foundations discussed earlier. Chapter 2 studies substitutes from two angles. It treats exact substitutes in the Arrow-Hurwicz theory, in which goods are assumed to be divisible, and the closely related Kelso-Crawford labor market theory, in which workers can work for only one firm, that is, they are "indivisible." It also treats the knapsack problem and Dantzig's "greedy" approximation algorithm, in which goods would be substitutes if only they were divisible. An auction that highlights the substitute aspect generates prices that are good guides to decision making.

Chapter 3 returns to the foundations of auction theory, studying Vickrey auctions, with special attention to the case of goods that are substitutes. In the general case, what distinguishes the Vickrey auction is that it selects efficient outcomes and is strategy-proof. In the substitutes case, it also finds prices that are "competitive" in a suitable sense, so that the auctioneer does not pay too much for what it acquires. Chapter 4 studies extensions of these ideas to cases when the computations required by the Vickrey auction are too difficult, and particularly how computational, incentive, and investment ideas came together in the design of the FCC's 2016 incentive auction. Chapter 5 summarizes what I have presented and suggests some new applications and new questions suggested by my analyses.

APPENDIX TO CHAPTER 1

A REPORT ON THE FCC INCENTIVE AUCTION

The FCC Incentive Auction began at 6 p.m. Eastern Time on March 29, 2016. That time marked the deadline for TV broadcasters that wished to participate in the auction to make legally binding commitments to relinquish their spectrum rights in exchange for the opening prices offered in the auction.

The major steps in the incentive auction are the following ones.

A1. TV BROADCASTERS' INITIAL COMMITMENTS

In this chapter, I focused on the option for UHF-TV station owners to relinquish all their rights and cease over-the-air broadcasting in exchange for a cash payment. But in the actual auction, broadcasters had multiple other options for which broadcast rights to relinquish. A UHF-TV station could relinquish its UHF license in exchange for a combination of cash and a VHF license at the same location in either the "high" or "low" part of the VHF band, denoted HVHF and LVHF, respectively. Or, an existing LVHF or HVHF station could offer to relinquish its rights in the auction to make space for a former UHF station. The auction system as described later set high opening prices, relying on competition to bring the opening prices down to a reasonable, competitive level.

Before making an initial commitment, each broadcaster reviewed the opening prices that the FCC posted for each option and decided which, if any, of the options it found acceptable. Opening prices were set generously to encourage broadcasters to participate, much above what the auctioneer expected the value of broadcast stations to be.

Details. The opening price for each station was determined by a formula, which set a price proportional to a value index for the station. The value index for a station was equal to $(XY)^{0.5}$, where X is the population in the station's service area and Y is the number of other stations with which that station might potentially interfere. Including X in the computation allowed the FCC to offer higher prices to stations in densely populated areas to encourage their participation, without raising the cost so high as to prevent any transactions from taking place. Y was included to give priority to clearing stations that might be particularly difficult to include in a new channel assignment. The sum of the opening prices for broadcasters agreeing to go off-air was a staggering $120 billion. For the options of switching to broadcast on HVHF or LVHF, the initial price offer was 40 percent or 75 percent, respectively, of the price offer to go off-air.

The VHF bands, consisting of broadcast channels 2–13, use lower frequencies than UHF and are generally regarded to be less desirable than the UHF band for television broadcasting. The auction offered separate prices for LVHF and HVHF bands. Existing VHF broadcasters could also participate. HVHF broadcasters could offer to relinquish their rights in exchange for cash or for a combination of cash and a license to use an LVHF channel. LVHF broadcasters could offer to relinquish their rights in exchange for cash.

A2. SETTING THE CLEARING TARGET FOR THE FIRST STAGE

One of the jobs of the incentive auction was to determine how many channels should remain devoted to UHF-TV broadcast and how many should be switched to mobile broadband use. As described in more detail later, the auction process began by setting an initial, very high quantity target, equal to the maximum number of channels that could possibly be cleared. This number of channels would, if necessary, be reduced in additional stages. To determine where to start the process, the FCC used the information from the initial commitments. It computed the maximum number of channels that could possibly be made available for mobile broadband on a near-nationwide level if it were eventually to accept offers from all of the participating broadcasters, the FCC determining that it could potentially clear 126 MHz of TV spectrum, which is 21 UHF-TV channels.

That computation fixed the initial clearing target and meant that twenty-one fewer channels would be available for over-the-air UHF-TV broadcast, but the spectrum that could be offered for sale to the broadband providers would be somewhat less. After subtracting the bandwidth needed to establish guard bands between uplink and downlink uses of the spectrum, between TV broadcast and mobile broadband uses, and around channel 37 (which is reserved for radio astronomy and medical telemetry), that would leave 100 MHz of spectrum for mobile broadband use.

Details. The optimization involved in setting the actual target is subtle. While the ideal would be to have the same frequencies available in every part of the country, imposing that goal as a constraint would be too limiting. For example, treaty constraints operating along the Mexican border are particularly costly, substantially limiting the ability to clear many channels in the highly populated San Diego area. In other areas, near-perfect clearing can be achieved by judiciously assigning broadcast rights to a TV station in frequencies in the guard band, resulting in small impairments to the broadband service. The auction was designed to allow small amounts of impairments in the licenses to be sold. Licenses that are deemed to be significantly impaired were regarded as a separate product, to be sold at a lower price. In the actual calculation, the initial clearing target for the San Diego area involved only 50 MHz of spectrum dedicated to broadband. Among the broadband licenses offered for sale, impairments resulting from TV broadcasts in the guard bands affected less than 1 percent of the U.S. population.

A3. REVERSE-AUCTION BIDDING

Once the initial clearing target had been set, the reverse auction to purchase television broadcast rights could begin. In some areas of the United States, there were more stations willing to relinquish their rights than were needed to achieve the clearing target. The reverse auction was a descending-price auction in which these stations competed against one another in a series of rounds, offering their broadcast rights at successively lower prices, so long as the government did not need to acquire those rights to meet its current clearing target. A station's price stopped declining when the clearing target was unreachable without acquiring that station. Thus, each individual station could, in principle, have a different price.

The first round of the reverse auction took place on May 31, 2016. When the auction for this clearing target had ended, the total price offered to all stations to achieve the initial clearing target was $86.22 billion—down from the opening price but still a huge amount. Subsequent stages of the auction with lower clearing targets will lead to lower prices before the auction can end.

Details. The initial clearing target is set equal to the maximum number of channels that could be cleared using the bids of *all* the participating stations. While it is likely that, in some areas of the country, there are more bids than needed to achieve the target, the objective ensures that there will be other areas in which the auctioneer can achieve the target only by actually purchasing rights from all of the stations that offer to relinquish them. In those areas, the stations face no competition, so the prices are never reduced from the generous opening prices. If there are many such areas, then the reverse-auction bidding of the first stage would end with many stations being offered their opening prices.

A4. FORWARD-AUCTION BIDDING

In the forward auction, mobile broadband providers compete to acquire licenses to use particular frequencies in the spectrum. While TV broadcast licenses each involved a bandwidth of 6 MHz in a particular frequency over the area that could be served by broadcast equipment, mobile broadband licenses were very different. Each license entailed a right to use 5 MHz of spectrum for an uplink signal and 5 MHz for a downlink signal in particular frequencies: 10 MHz in total for each license. The United States was divided into 416 "partial economic areas" (PEAs)—geographic areas smaller than the traditional "economic areas" that had been used for licenses in some earlier auction sales. For each PEA, each license could be designated as either a category 1 or a category 2 license. Category 1 licenses were those for which no more than 15 percent of the population in the PEA resided in areas that would be unserviceable using that license (due to interference with some television broadcast). About 97 percent of the licenses offered in the auction were in category 1. About 99 percent of those had *zero* impairment, meaning that 100 percent of the population in the area could be served. The remaining licenses are category 2 licenses. For the forward auction, bidders did not bid on a particular license, but on a "product," which is a group of licenses described by the PEA and category.

In principle, the forward and reverse auctions could be conducted in parallel. In practice, however, the operational demands on the FCC would be too great. Staff need to manage and oversee the forward and reverse auctions, to run seminars and train bidders to use the software, to answer bidders' many questions, and to make sure that all of the many systems for registration, security, and bidding are operating properly. Doing all that for such complex auctions and switching attention between two quite different sets of rules would have been too challenging. The forward auction began only after the reverse auction had ended. Bidding in the forward auction began on August 16, 2016.

The forward auction was conducted in a series of rounds. It was a "clock auction," meaning that the auctioneer specified a separate price for each product and the bidders responded by naming the quantities that they demanded. Prices are increased for any product for which demand exceeds supply, and bidders are prevented from reducing their demand for any product by so much that demand falls below supply. The forward auction ends when there is no longer excess demand for any product.

This auction structure resembles what the nineteenth-century French economist Léon Walras had called a *tatonnement*, in which prices rise or fall separately for products according to whether demand for each exceeds or falls short of the supply for that product. The most significant differences are the constraints that limit the quantities that bidders can name. The constraints on bidders are these:

First, a bidder may not reduce its demand for a product for which the price is not currently increasing. This helps to ensure that a bid is a serious offer for each product, contributing to the integrity of the auction. However, as I describe further in later chapters, this rule can prevent straightforward bidding by a bidder that does not regard different licenses as substitutes.

Second, no bidder may increase its overall activity from round to round (the "activity rule"). This rules out strategies in which bidders wait to see how the prices are developing before placing serious bids and so provides some assurance that the auction moves forward at some minimum pace, at least in its early rounds.[9]

Third, a bidder's total activity in the first round of the auction is limited by the up-front cash deposit that it makes. Up-front deposits help to ensure that bidders will eventually pay the prices they have bid or else face sanctions, including a forfeit of the deposits they have made.

Details. The design of lots and products is one of the most neglected questions in the economic theory of auctions, and the FCC's choices in this case are suggestive of at least some of the issues. Licenses that cover partial economic areas were adopted as a compromise based on comments from the stakeholders. Some companies, especially rural telephone companies, wished to bid for licenses that they could use to improve service in the areas surrounding cities, without having to buy spectrum to serve the cities themselves. The relatively small PEAs make that possible. However, because some previous licenses had been sold covering larger "economic areas" and some companies wanted to enhance their services in existing areas, the areas needed to be defined so that a group of them could be combined to serve a full economic area.

An important innovation in this auction is the "conditional reserve." As explained later, for this auction to succeed, the FCC needed to raise enough revenue in the forward auction to cover the costs of the reverse auction. However, the FCC also wanted to prevent the largest incumbents from foreclosing competition by acquiring nearly all of this high-quality spectrum. The solution was the conditional reserve rule, according to which all bidders would bid on an equal footing until the forward auction met a certain revenue threshold. After that, if certain "reserve qualified bidders" were bidding to acquire licenses in a PEA, then some of those licenses would become unavailable for acquisition by incumbent providers in that area. They would become a new product in the auction, which was available for bidding only by qualified bidders. The intent of this rule was to allow competition to raise sufficient revenue without allowing incumbents to foreclose competition in the wireless market.

In commenting on the rules for this auction, the consultants for AT&T recommended a particular kind of combinatorial bidding. The Vickrey auction that I describe later in this monograph is a combinatorial auction, and other designs may be attractive too, especially when the lots for sale are not substitutes. In the incentive auction, it appears that although the substitutes condition is unlikely to hold exactly, there is reason to think it may hold approximately, and no evidence that it fails badly. So, the case for a novel and complex combinatorial design was too weak to sway the decision makers.

One innovation that was implemented is the use of "intra-round bidding." In a multiround auction without intra-round bidding, a bidder that has been demanding four units of a product at the price *P* that prevailed after the last round might specify that it wants to reduce its demand to two units at the price for the next round, which might be 5 percent higher. With intra-round bidding, the bidder could instead specify that it wants to reduce its demand during the round at some in-between prices. For example, it might reduce demand to three units when the price has increased by 2 percent and to two units when the price has increased by 4 percent. Conceptually, the auction algorithm stops the price increases when demand falls just equal to supply for each product. The actual price-setting algorithm involves some additional subtleties, because a bidder who reduces its demand for one product may be eligible to increase its demand for another product.

A5. FINAL-STAGE RULE AND ADDITIONAL STAGES

Once a clearing target has been set and the reverse and forward auctions completed, the revenues and costs are compared. If the revenues from the forward auction meet a minimum absolute standard, and if they are high enough to pay the cost of clearing broadcasters as determined by the reverse auction, then the whole procedure ends. This determination is called the "final stage rule."

If, instead, the revenues are insufficient, the clearing target is reduced and another auction stage is initiated. In practice, the initial clearing target was twenty-one channels (and ten forward-auction licenses in each PEA covering a total of 100 MHz of spectrum bandwidth). If a second stage becomes necessary, then the clearing target for the second stage of the actual FCC auction would be nineteen channels (and 90 MHz of forward-auction licenses). Subsequent stages will involve still lower clearing targets.

At the new auction stage, prices and allocations begin where the previous stage left off. The first-stage prices are ones at which the FCC could acquire enough broadcast rights to clear twenty-one channels, but in subsequent stages the FCC no longer needs to clear so many stations, so it can reduce the prices it offers. Buying fewer stations at lower prices brings down the cost in two ways. Meanwhile, in the forward auction, supplies would be reduced, but prices would continue to increase.

A6. THE EXTENDED ROUND

It is possible that when bidding in the forward auction ends for some clearing target, the prices fall short of meeting the revenue target by a small amount, say by less than 20 percent. Conceivably, rather than going through another stage with higher prices and fewer licenses, the winning bidders for the stage would prefer to see the auction prices increase to achieve clearing in the current stage rather than wait for another round, when prices would increase anyway and the quantity of spectrum available for sale would be reduced. The "extended round" is the name given to an additional clock round in which prices can increase by up to 20 percent to achieve market clearing. If the bidders choose to continue bidding for their current quantities of licenses as prices increase, then the current stage can become the last one, and the current clearing target is achieved.

A7. THE ASSIGNMENT ROUNDS

Once the final stage rule has been satisfied and winners are determined in the forward and reverse auctions, the final allocation is still not completely determined. The main reason is that the licenses in each category do not specify the actual frequencies that the wireless broadband companies will use. Some bidders may have preferences about that assignment. For example, efficient network operation requires that carriers with multiple licenses in one PEA should have those on adjacent frequencies, and there may also be efficiencies in a single carrier having the same frequencies in adjacent PEAs. Carriers are sometimes concerned about harmonics, preferring certain frequencies because of systems operating on nonadjacent frequencies.

All of these preferences are taken into account in the assignment rounds, in which the bidders bid in a series of rounds for the combinations of frequencies they wish to acquire in each PEA where they are already winners. The assignment rules guarantee that each winner will be assigned adjacent frequencies in each area, and the bids made in the assignment rounds determine a final allocation of frequencies, which is consistent with the final product assignment determined in the other rounds of the auction.

There is also work to do to determine the assignment of the broadcasters after the reverse auction. The algorithm used during the auction ensures only that some feasible assignment of remaining stations to channels exists. After the auction, the best assignment of stations to channels still needs to be determined. The main objective for that assignment is to minimize the cost of retuning stations, for example, by allowing some stations to continue to broadcast on their preauction channel.

As we go to press, the FCC incentive auction has completed stage 2, in which the clearing target was reduced from 126 MHz of broadcast spectrum and 100 MHz of wireless spectrum to 114 MHz of broadcast spectrum and 90 MHz of wireless spectrum. Before the auction ends, there will be subsequent stages with still lower clearing targets.

This description of the incentive auction highlights the gap between standard economic models and the practice of auction market design. A central theme of this chapter—that each individual product may be distinct—appears in a couple of places in the preceding description.

- In the forward auction for selling mobile broadband licenses, the products are divided into two categories, corresponding to whether interference is more or less than 15 percent. Notice that no attempt is made to vary products to have exactly the same amounts of interference. Partly to remedy that, the assignment rounds are included, allowing bidders to vary the prices of individual licenses within a category. But the assignment rounds do more, for even when there is virtually no difference in the amounts of interference, a bidder's values for two sets of licenses covering the same territory may still depend on whether they use adjacent frequencies, whether they use the same frequencies as the bidder's licenses in adjacent territories, and whether their harmonics may interfere with the effective use of distant frequencies operated by the same bidder.

- In the reverse auction, every station is treated as unique. Each has its own price, based on its characteristics and on a complex computation about the channels to which it may be assigned without creating interference for other broadcasters.

Less obvious in the FCC design are the product design decisions (or the "lots" in the auction), which are rarely even mentioned in economic theory. These decisions are invisible in the description above, because the products are already defined when the process begins. Here are two examples of such decisions made in the context of the incentive auction.

- In the forward auction, the broadband licenses offered for sale are "paired licenses," in which two frequencies are provided, one for uplink from the device to a cell site and the other for downlink back to the device. This structure is ideal for use with "frequency division duplex" (FDD) wireless technology, but not for the alternative "time division duplex" (TDD) technology. That technology, which is used in China and Japan, alternately communicates uplink and downlink messages in short bursts and does not need or make good use of separated frequency bands. The 2009 U.K. auction for L-band spectrum (1452–1492 MHz) incorporated the possibility of competition between technologies, adding complexity to the auction design.

- In the reverse auction, UHF stations must relinquish their broadcast rights entirely to be compensated, either with cash or with a combination of cash and a VHF license. An alternative would be to allow the auctioneer to acquire other rights from a broadcaster. For example, the broadcaster might be compensated to accept a reduction in its interference-free broadcast area. The reasons to reject this alternative included its complexity for bidders and the greater computational complexity it would entail.

2

(NEAR-)SUBSTITUTES, PRICES, AND STABILITY

Formal economic theory is mathematical. It lists explicitly its primitive concepts (ones that are not defined in terms of other concepts), introduces notation to represent those, uses that notation to state its assumptions precisely, and finally derives some logical implications. The new material in this book is formal economic theory in that sense. To put the new theory in context, we review some older theories too, but not in complete detail, relying instead on interpretive accounts. Readers are referred to standard economics textbooks to find the missing details.

Neoclassical equilibrium theory represents the most important point of departure for our new account. That theory highlights the role of market-clearing prices in supporting the efficient allocation of resources. Among its most important assumptions are that each consumer cares only about his or her own individual consumption and that each firm's output is limited only by the resources that it uses.

The principal findings of the theory are summarized by three theorems, as follows:

- The *first welfare theorem* asserts that any resource allocation consistent with competitive equilibrium is Pareto efficient. This means that any feasible allocation that is more preferred by some consumer is less preferred by some other consumer. As is standard in economics, we use the unmodified word "efficient" to mean "Pareto efficient."
- The *competitive equilibrium existence theorem* identifies sufficient conditions under which competitive equilibrium outcomes can be guaranteed to exist. We will not explore the conditions here, but our models will examine whether a similar conclusion may hold under a different set of assumptions that are more relevant for the problems we will study.
- The *second welfare theorem* asserts that under the same conditions identified by the competitive equilibrium existence theorem, any efficient allocation is the competitive equilibrium allocation corresponding to some allocation of property rights.

These celebrated theorems provide a beautiful formal account of some of the central ideas that Adam Smith first presented informally in his 1776 classic, *The Wealth of Nations*. Part of the backdrop for Smith's book was the idea that, with the decline of feudalism, there would be no lord to direct workers. How would anyone know whether to plant fields, shoe horses, or tailor clothing? The existence theorem says that if the right prices are found, then just enough of each kind of product will be supplied to fulfill demand exactly! The first welfare theorem adds that if some prices can be found, then the result is a Pareto-efficient outcome. This means that the allocation is nonwasteful in a very particular sense: any other feasible allocation that some consumer prefers must be less preferred by another consumer. It is not possible to rearrange production and distribution so that *all* consumers are better off. The second welfare theorem adds that if one prefers a different efficient outcome, perhaps on grounds of distribution or equity, then it is conceptually possible to rearrange the ownership shares of different consumers so that the market outcome coincides with the preferred outcome.

While these theorems achieve a great deal, they also leave much unresolved. They do not say how competitive equilibrium prices might come to prevail in a decentralized economic system, or even that competitive equilibrium prices are unique. If there are many market-clearing prices, the predictions that the theory is able to make are correspondingly weaker.

Adam Smith had suggested a mechanism in his original account, which led to further developments in the theory. Expressed in modern terms, Smith's idea was that if there is more demand than supply for a good, producers will find that they can raise their prices, which tends both to reduce demand and to encourage producers to make more of the good. However, changing the price of one good may also affect demand for another, so it is hardly obvious how this dynamic process will play out. Does it lead to the emergence of prices that clear all the markets? Is there a unique such vector of prices? Léon Walras formalized the main questions of competitive equilibrium theory in his book *Elements of Pure Economics*, first published in 1874. Included in his analysis was the procedure that he called the *tatonnement*, in which prices of goods with *excess demand*, meaning goods for which demand minus supply is positive, would rise, and prices of goods with *excess supply* (for which demand minus supply is negative) would fall.

In 1959 Kenneth Arrow and Leo Hurwicz made important headway on this project. They studied the case of goods that are *gross substitutes*, which means that increasing the price of one good can never reduce demand for another. They showed there is a unique competitive equilibrium price vector in that case, and regardless of the initial prices, the Walrasian *tatonnement* price adjustment procedure leads prices to evolve in a way that eventually converges to the unique market-clearing prices.

In market design problems, the goal is not to set prices for all goods in the economy but just for the subset of goods for which a market is to be created. For such problems, the Arrow-Hurwicz analysis sets the context too broadly, and the idea of a Walrasian *tatonnement* procedure needs to be narrowed and replaced by an auction procedure for just the subset of goods, with the prices of all other goods remaining unchanged. In the auction modeled later, prices for the relevant goods start low enough that there is excess demand for each. The intuitive idea is that prices get bid up when there is excess demand for a good, so the model assumes that prices are increasing in that case, just as they do in the Walrasian *tatonnement*.

2.1 SUBSTITUTES, PRICES, AND STABILITY IN A NEOCLASSICAL MODEL

As explained earlier, since my focus here is on market design, I omit some aspects of the original Arrow-Hurwicz model, namely that all goods' prices can change and that all goods are substitutes. The cost of this omission is that the conclusion that there are unique market-clearing prices is lost. Nevertheless, much remains, and the ideas that Arrow and Hurwicz introduced have important implications for auction analysis, as illustrated in figure 2.1.

Figure 2.1 illustrates a hypothetical world in which one good—called the "numeraire"—plays a special role. It is used as the unit for expressing prices. For example, prices may be expressed in terms of ounces of gold or bushels of wheat.

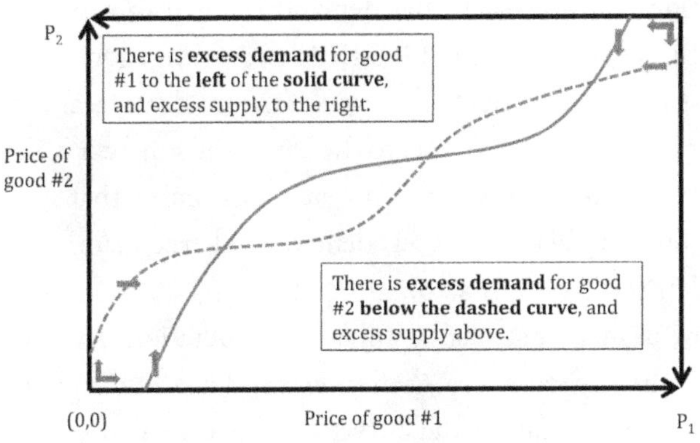

Figure 2.1 When goods are "gross substitutes," auction dynamics direct prices up from (0, 0) toward the low-price competitive equilibrium, or down from (P_1, P_2) to the high-price competitive equilibrium.

To keep the graph manageable, our hypothetical world includes just two other goods besides the numeraire; these are labeled good 1 and good 2. In a primitive economy, they might be wheat and corn. In a more advanced economy, they might be amounts of radio spectrum bandwidth at two different frequencies. The logic illustrated in the figure for two goods can be extended to any larger number of goods. I allow later that the net demand for each good can depend on both prices. For example, if the price of wheat goes up, consumers might buy less wheat and more corn. I assume, however, that the strict *law of demand* applies, which means that the net demand for each good is decreasing in the price of that good. This might happen because an increase in the price of wheat may prompt buyers to purchase less wheat or sellers to supply more wheat or both.

Figure 2.1 has the prices of the two goods on the two axes. It displays two curves. The solid curve represents the combination of prices such that demand is equal to supply for good 1. Since net demand is strictly decreasing, good 1 is in excess supply at points to the right of the solid curve, and it is in excess demand for points to the left of the solid curve. The figure embeds the assumption that on the curve that forms the boundary between excess demand and excess supply, the net demand is exactly zero.

The dashed curve has a similar interpretation. At points below the dashed curve, there is excess demand for good 2, while at points above the curve, there is excess supply. For simplicity, assume that both curves are continuous.

Besides the law of demand, the analysis uses three additional assumptions that restrict the boundaries and shapes of the two curves. First, when one price is sufficiently close to zero, there is excess demand for the low-priced good. Thus, the solid curve hits the horizontal axis at a positive price, and the dashed curve hits the vertical axis at a positive price. Second, for each good, at its maximum price in the graph, the good is so expensive that there is excess supply: either buyers stop buying or sellers increase supply when the price, in terms of the numeraire, become sufficiently high. So, the solid curve hits the upper boundary of the box and the dashed curve hits the right-hand boundary. With these assumptions, it is clear that the two curves must cross somewhere. Formally, that conclusion is a consequence of the intermediate value theorem. The point at which the curves cross is on both curves, so it is a pair of prices with neither excess supply nor excess demand for either good. At those prices, supply equals demand for both goods.

The third assumption is that the nonnumeraire goods are gross substitutes. This leads to a property of figure 2.1—the two curves slope upward, never downward. Combined with the law-of-demand assumption that increasing the price of good 1 reduces the net demand for that good, such a price increase can leave the net demand at zero only if the price for good 2 increases as well. That explains why the solid curve slopes upward, and a symmetric argument applies to the dashed curve.

The gross substitutes condition is a reasonable one for many market design problems. For example, in a market for coffee beans, increasing the price of Kenyan beans is likely to increase demand for Rwandan beans, as buyers substitute cheaper beans for more expensive ones. Still, there are plentiful examples of goods that are not substitutes. For example, if airline flights to Honolulu become more expensive, one might expect the demand for Hawaiian hotels to fall. Flights and hotels are complements, because travelers who buy one typically buy the other. There are still more possibilities. Some goods may act like substitutes in some price ranges but like complements in others, meaning that the effect of a price increase for good 1 on the demand for good 2 may not be monotonic. For example, raising the price of gasoline up to some point may increase the demand for fuel-efficient cars, but a further significant price increase might lead consumers to increase carpooling or make greater use of public transportation, which then reduces the demand for all kinds of cars.

The figure, which incorporates our assumptions, also illustrates our main conclusions. The first, already mentioned, is that any two curves with the properties discussed earlier must necessarily intersect. So, there must exist at least one pair of prices at which supply is equal to demand for both goods at the same time. In the figure, there are three such price pairs.[1]

A second conclusion is that among these market-clearing price vectors, there is one price vector that is lowest in every coordinate and one that is highest in every coordinate. Indeed, every market-clearing price vector lies on the solid curve, and all the points on that curve are ordered from lowest to highest, so the lowest crossing must be lowest in both components.[2]

The next conclusion concerns how prices evolve dynamically in a decentralized market and, relatedly, how prices develop in a multiproduct auction.

In a *tatonnement* like the one Arrow and Hurwicz described, prices $P(t)$ vary continuously as a function of time. Suppose that the prices for both goods start low (in the lower left corner of the figure), and let us examine how the prices might evolve. With low prices for both goods, there is excess demand for both, so both prices begin to rise. During the price adjustment, if prices ever reach the solid curve, there will then be zero excess demand for good 1, so that price stops increasing, at least temporarily. This implies that the prices $P(t)$ can never cross the solid curve and, similarly, cannot cross the dashed curve. The prices can only increase and cannot stop until $P(t)$ reaches the lowest point of crossing of the two curves, which is the lowest market-clearing price vector. One needs to add an assumption to ensure that the process does not slow down so much that it stalls, but subject to that, the conclusion is that $P(t)$ converges monotonically up to the lowest market-clearing price vector.

A similar analysis applies when both prices start high, say in the upper right for figure 2.1. The price vector $P(t)$ then converges monotonically down to the highest market-clearing price vector.

With market design in mind, this analysis implies that when goods are substitutes, an auction in which prices move in just one direction—either monotonically upward or monotonically downward—can locate market-clearing prices. An ascending auction—in which prices for both goods start low and each price increases gradually so long as there is excess demand for the corresponding good—can arrive at the lowest equilibrium price vector. Similarly, a descending auction—in which prices for both goods start high and each price gradually falls when there is excess supply of that good—can arrive at the highest equilibrium price vector.

To summarize, our findings in this section assert that under the assumptions described (the law of demand applies, there is excess demand at low prices and excess supply at high prices, and the nonnumeraire goods are gross substitutes), the following conclusions apply:

- Market-clearing price vectors exist. These are price vectors that lead to zero excess demand for each good.
- Among the market-clearing price vectors, there is a lowest one, with the property that the price for each good is no higher than the corresponding price for any other market-clearing price vector. There is also a highest market-clearing price vector, which similarly has a weakly higher price for every good than any other market-clearing price vector.
- An ascending auction, modeled as a continuous process in which each good's price starts low and has a positive rate of increase only when the good is in excess demand, converges monotonically upward to the lowest market-clearing price vector. A similar statement applies to auctions that start with high prices and decrease when there is excess supply, converging to the highest market-clearing price vector.

2.2 SUBSTITUTES, PRICES, AND STABILITY WITH DISCRETE GOODS

Although the original Arrow-Hurwicz model assumed that goods are divisible, the analysis described earlier is performed using only a price graph, making no reference to any assumption that goods are divisible. One may wonder: Is the assumption of divisible goods used in the argument? If so, can some version of the same analysis nevertheless apply to indivisible goods like cars and houses?

To answer the first question, recall that we assumed that demand for a good is a strictly decreasing function of its price. That cannot be true for a good that is sold in discrete quantities, and it implies that the set of points where excess demand is zero is generally not a curve. If the good in question were a house or another indivisible good, then the sets of prices at which demand is equal to supply would often be "thick" curves, as demand must sometimes remain unchanged as prices vary. Moreover, there would be boundary issues: as the price of a good increases so that the quantity demanded falls discretely from, say, one unit to zero, there must be some price at which the consumer is just indifferent. There is some highest price that a rational consumer would pay for, say, a Hawaiian vacation package, but at which the consumer would be equally happy just to switch to an alternative vacation option. When it is possible that two choices are both optimal for the consumer, then demand can no longer be represented accurately by a single-valued function.

As argued later, although these technical differences are real, they do not much affect the main conclusions, and they can be accommodated with only modest changes to the analysis and main conclusions. The core ideas used in the preceding analysis also remain largely unchanged, although the details we introduce to accommodate the differences introduce some economically superficial differences.

Kelso and Crawford (1982) were the first to explore such an extension of the theory to discrete goods. They modeled a labor market in which the demand was not for goods, but for workers in a finite set I. They assumed that workers cannot split their time among firms. Demand came from business firms in a finite set J. Each firm seeks to hire workers based on how well they fit the firm's needs and how much they cost. The mathematical model that I use here is based closely on theirs.

Let W denote the set of possible wages that any firm can offer when hiring any worker. A worker generally cares both about the identity of the firm that employs him or her and about the wage he or she is paid. Given the identity of the firm, the worker always prefers a higher wage to a lower one. Mathematically, a *contract* is a triple (i, j, w_i^j) that specifies the identities of the worker i and the firm j and the wage w_i^j that firm j will pay to worker i. We denote the event that worker i does not work for any firm by the symbol $\varnothing_i$. It is convenient to refer to $\varnothing_i$ as a contract as well, so the set of possible contracts is $(I \times J \times W) \cup \{\varnothing_i \mid i \in I\}$.

It will be convenient later to enumerate the possible wages, so I assume that the set W is finite. Thus, each worker i can limit attention to the $|J| \times |W| + 1$ possible contracts that may result from his or her participation in the job market: he or she may be hired by a firm $j \in J$ at a wage $w_i^j \in W$, or he or she may remain unemployed. We assume that each worker can rank these alternatives strictly: he or she is not indifferent between any two possible contracts. We say that a contract is *acceptable* for worker i if he or she strictly prefers that contract to $\varnothing_i$.

Analogous to workers, firms care both about the identities of the employees they hire and the wages they must pay. However, unlike workers, firms can enter into several contracts to hire multiple workers, and they may care about the mix. For example, a department store might want to hire someone who will be a salesperson and someone who will be an aesthetician, and some workers may be qualified for both kinds of jobs. In general, a firm has preferences over the set of contracts that it makes. Given the finite set of worker-wage pairs that firm j may consider, there is also a finite number of subsets, so it is reasonable and convenient to assume that the firm is never indifferent between any two subsets. In particular, for any possible vector w giving a wage for each worker, each firm j can identify a unique best set of workers $D^j(w)$ to hire. A crucial and more restrictive assumption about firms' demand is that workers are *gross substitutes*. Informally, this means that raising wages for one or more workers k never diminishes the firm's demand for another worker i whose wage has remained unchanged. Formally, the restriction is the following one:

Definition

Workers are gross substitutes for firm j, if for all $w^j \in W^I$, $k \neq i$ and $w'^j_k > w^j_k, i \in D^j(w^j) \Rightarrow i \in D^j(w'^j_k, w^j_{-k})$.[3]

2.2.1 FACILITATING COMPARISONS

Write $W = \{\hat{w}_1, \ldots, \hat{w}_N\}$ and number the wages in ascending order: $\hat{w}_1 < \cdots < \hat{w}_N$.

To facilitate comparison with the Arrow-Hurwicz model, we also introduce two extra wages into the model. One, $\hat{w}_{N+1} > \hat{w}_N$, is so high that no firm would pay it and any worker would accept it. The second, $\hat{w}_0 < \hat{w}_1$, is so low that no worker would accept it and any firm would offer it. These wages are the analogues to the very high and very low prices used earlier in this chapter, for which there was always excess supply or excess demand. We use $\overline{W} = W \cup \{\hat{w}_0, \hat{w}_{N+1}\}$ to denote this extended set of wages.

For our formal analysis, it is convenient to identify the next higher wage and next lower wage using functions n and p, defined as follows: $n(\hat{w}_m) = \hat{w}_{m+1}$ (the *next* wage, which is defined for wages in $\overline{W}$ less than $\hat{w}_{N+1}$), and $p(\hat{w}_m) = \hat{w}_{m-1}$ (the *previous* wage, which is defined for wages in $\overline{W}$ greater than $\hat{w}_0$).

2.2.2 MATCHING DEFINITIONS AND NOTATION

To describe the outcome of the labor market, we introduce the notion of a matching. Informally, this is just a consistent collection of contracts C, in which there is at most one contract for each worker i. If there is a contract in C between worker i and firm j, then we say that i is matched to j, and we use C^j to denote the set of contracts associated with firm j. The corresponding formal statement is as follows:

Definitions

1. A *matching* is a set of contracts C such that (i) for each worker i, there is at most one contract $(i, j, w_i^j) \in C$, and (ii) if there is no such contract, then $\varnothing_i \in C$. (Thus, for each worker, there is exactly one corresponding element of C.)
2. If $(i, j, w_i^j) \in C$, then we say that worker i and firm j are *matched* in C.
3. We say that i is *unmatched* in C if $\varnothing_i$ in C.
4. $C^j \overset{\text{def}}{=} \{(i, j', w_i^{j'}) \in C \mid j' = j\}$.

We also use the following definitions, with corresponding informal statements.

Definitions

1. A matching C is *blocked* by the contract (i, j, w_i^j) if (i) worker i strictly prefers (i, j, w_i^j) to $(i, j', w_i^{j'}) \in C$, and (ii) there is some set of contracts $S \subseteq C^j \cup \{(i, j, w_i^j)\}$ such that j strictly prefers S to the set C^j.
2. A matching C is *unstable* if either of two conditions holds:
   a. There is some $(i, j, w_i^j) \in C$ such that either (i) worker i prefers $\varnothing_i$ to $(i, j, w_i^j) \in C$, or (ii) firm j prefers $C^j - \{(i, j, w_i^j)\}$ to C^j, or
   b. C is blocked by some worker-firm-wage triple (i, j, w_i^j).
3. A matching C is *stable* if it is not unstable.

For definition 1, informally, a matching is blocked by a worker-firm pair (i, j) if there is some contract that i and j would both strictly prefer to sign instead of settling for what is prescribed by the matching C. For the worker, the condition involved is quite straightforward: it means that i prefers the alternative contract to the one prescribed by the matching. For the firm, however, the condition is more subtle, because the firm must consider what it will do with its other contracts if it signs the proposed contract with worker i. In the definition, firm j considers whether (i) to sign the alternative contract with worker i while also keeping some or all of its other contracts, so that it signs the set of contracts S, or (ii) to reject the proposed contract with worker i and just keep the set of contracts C^j prescribed by the matching.

For definition 2, informally, there are two ways for a matching to be unstable: it can be rejected by some unsatisfied individual worker or firm or blocked by some worker-firm pair. The first case happens when there is some worker i who finds his or her contract to be unacceptable: he or she prefers to be unemployed rather than to take this contract with firm j. It can also happen when there is some firm j that prefers to omit worker i and settle for the smaller set of workers rather than to accept this contract with i. The second case is that the matching may be blocked by a worker-firm pair, as described earlier. If the matching is not unstable in any of these ways, then it is stable.

2.2.3 CONNECTIONS TO ARROW AND HURWICZ

The connection between stable matching and market equilibrium lies hidden in the standard formulation that we have described, because the two formulations seem so different. In market equilibrium, decisions are made by individuals, and a price and allocation fail the test of equilibrium if some individual wants to change his or her demand, buying or selling something more or different than is prescribed. A matching, as formulated earlier, can be unstable because it is blocked by a worker-firm pair rather than by an individual. How can these two seemingly different approaches be reconciled?

Informally, the reconciliation involves two main ideas. One is to characterize the stable matching conditions in a new way. For our informal treatment, let us focus exclusively on the most problematic part: the characterization of a blocking contract. In order for a blocking contract involving worker i and firm j to exist, the parties must be able to find some wage such that the resulting contract is preferred by both. Turning that condition around, there can be no blocking contract involving worker i and firm j if there is some wage w_i^j such that the firm j is unwilling to pay that much and worker i is unwilling to accept anything less. This formulation converts the problem of proving that there is no wage that is acceptable to both parties into a problem of finding some wage that satisfies the conditions just described.

The second main idea is to reformulate our description of the market outcome using more prices (wages) than just the ones written into the contracts the parties actually signed: we also include wages for all the other pairs to characterize the offers that might have been made and rejected among pairs that never became matched. To achieve that, I introduce the notion of an augmented matching (w, C), where C is a matching and $w = (w_i^j)_{i=1,\ldots,|I|}^{j=1,\ldots,|J|}$ specifies the missing wages. I emphasize again that this includes not just the wages for matched pairs, but wages for every worker-firm pair.

The formal ideas are introduced first, and the informal discussion follows.

Definitions

1. An augmented matching is a pair (w, C) such that $(i, j, \overline{w}_i^j) \in C \Rightarrow w_i^j = \overline{w}_i^j$.
2. An augmented matching (w, C) is *stable* if
    a. for each firm j, $D^j(w^j) = \{i : (i, j, w_i^j) \in C^j\}$,
    b. if $\varnothing_i \in C$, then i prefers $\varnothing_i$ to each element of $\{(i, j, p(w_i^j)) | j \in J\}$, and
    c. if $\varnothing_i \notin C$, then i prefers $(i, j, w_i^j) \in C$ to each element of $\{(i, j', p(w_i^{j'})) | j' \neq j\} \cup \{\varnothing_i\}$.

In the first definition, as already discussed, an augmented matching (w, C) expands the standard notion of a matching by adding wages for all worker-firm pairs. Some care is needed here, however, because C already includes wages for the worker-firm pairs that are matched. The "such that" condition in the definition of augmented matching requires that the two wage specifications must coincide.

The second definition formalizes the intuitive idea described earlier. Informally, it says that the augmented matching is stable if the matching specifies that each firm j will hire the workers it most prefers at the prevailing wages, and that each worker is choosing his or her most preferred contract, assuming that the other firms, with whom he or she is not matched, would be unwilling to pay as much as w_i^j.

Although the definitions of stability for stable matchings and stable augmented matchings are quite different in form, they are closely connected. (Recall in the following our notation $\bar{W} \stackrel{\text{def}}{=} \{\hat{w}_0, \ldots, \hat{w}_{N+1}\}$.)

Proposition 2.1

The matching C is stable if and only if there exist wages $w \in \bar{W}^{|I|\times|J|}$ such that the augmented matching (w, C) is stable.

Proof

Suppose that a matching C is stable. We must show that there exist wages for the pairs that are not matched such that (w,C) is stable. For any worker-firm pair (i, j) that is not matched in C, let w_i^j be the lowest wage such that worker i prefers (i, j, w_i^j) to his or her match contract (which may be with another firm j', or $\varnothing_i$). Such a wage is guaranteed to exist because of the introduction of $\hat{w}_{N+1}$. The augmented matching (w, C) is stable because (i) condition 2a of the definition is satisfied by the absence of blocking pairs in C, and (ii) conditions 2b and 2c are satisfied by construction of w. Thus, every stable matching C is also part of a stable augmented matching (w, C).

For the converse, suppose that (w,C) is a stable augmented matching. We must show that C is not unstable, that is, that neither condition 2a nor 2b of the definitions of instability is satisfied. Condition 2a is not satisfied, because stability of (w, C) implies that any employed worker i in C prefers his or her contract to $\varnothing_i$ and that each firm demands its full allotment of workers from C. Condition 2b is not satisfied either, because stability of (w, C) means the wage in any blocking contract involving i and j would have to satisfy two contradictory conditions: it must both be at least w_i^j (to be preferred by worker i) and be no more than $p(w_i^j) < w_i^j$ (to be preferred by firm j). ■

The next step is to describe an auction procedure for clearing the labor market and to see how that may lead, under a gross substitutes condition similar to the one employed by Arrow and Hurwicz, to a stable augmented matching (w, C).

2.2.4 INFORMAL DESCRIPTION OF THE AUCTION

Informally, the process we describe is one in which each worker conducts his or her own individual ascending auction, inviting firms to bid for his or her services. Unlike an ordinary commodity auction, in which the bidder who offers the highest price always wins, the auctioneers in this case are workers who care about the identity of the buyer, who will become their employer. Consequently, our worker-auctioneers choose winners based on the most preferred contract rather than merely based on the highest wage offer. To keep matters simple, our rules specify that in each round t, there is just one wage that a firm j is permitted to offer to worker i, which we denote by $w_i^j(t)$. Of course, a firm may choose to make no new offer to any particular worker in some round of the auction. Thus, $w(t) = \left(w_i^j(t)\right)_{i \in I, j \in J}$ describes the wages that the firms *consider* offering in round t.

The vector of wages $w(t)$ describes the progress of the various auctions in much the same way that the vector of prices $P(t)$ describes the evolution of the market in the Arrow-Hurwicz model. There are differences in the models, too. In the older model, goods were divisible; prices were allowed to be any numbers in certain intervals; and the *tatonnement* price-adjustment process was represented as proceeding continuously in time. In the present auction model, all of those things are represented differently. Workers are indivisible and can work for just one firm or for none; prices (wages) are restricted to lie in a particular finite set; and the auction takes place in a discrete series of rounds, as noted in the following example.

The auction begins in round 1 with $w_i^j(1)=\hat{w}_1$ for all i and j: firms consider only the lowest possible offer in the first round. In every round t, each firm j makes job offers to workers in its most preferred set $D^j\left(w^j(t)\right)$ at the currently allowed wages, and it makes no offers to the workers not in its preferred set. Thus, in any round t, some workers may receive multiple job offers, some may receive a single offer, and still others may receive no offer at all.

Once offers are made, each worker evaluates all of the offers directed to him or her, considering both the wage and the identity of the offering firm. He or she applies his or her preference ranking, rejecting all offers that are less preferred than being unemployed. If he or she has any offers remaining after that, he or she holds onto the best one and rejects all the others. At the end of round t, each firm learns which of its offers were rejected. If worker i rejects firm j's offer, then j's potential wage offer for the next round is the next higher one: $w_i^j(t+1)=n\left(w_i^j(t)\right)$; otherwise, the potential offer for the next round remains unchanged from the current round: $w_i^j(t+1)=w_i^j(t)$.

2.2.5 FORMALITIES

Each worker i is endowed with a complete, transitive, antisymmetric binary preference relation over his or her possible contracts $\{(i,j,w_i^j) \mid j \in J, w_i^j \in \bar{W}\}$. Antisymmetry, in this context, means that the worker is not indifferent between any pair of distinct contracts. Fixing the firm, workers also prefer higher wages: if $w_i^j > w_i'^j$, then worker i strictly prefers (i,j,w_i^j) to $(i,j,w_i'^j)$.

To give interpretations to the analysis, we may think of each firm j as being characterized by its strict preference relation over feasible subsets S of the set of contracts $\{(i,j,w_i^j) \mid i \in I, w_i^j \in \bar{W}\}$. To be feasible for j, the set S can include at most one contract for each worker i. Just as workers prefer contracts with higher wages, firms prefer contracts with lower wages. Given any set of contracts from which to choose, a firm selects its most preferred, feasible subset. Given a vector of wages $w = (w_i^j)_{i \in I,\, j \in J}$, firm j's choice is described later using the demand function $D^j(w^j)$, which identifies the workers i associated with firm j's most preferred set of contracts from among $\{(i,j,w_i^j) \mid i \in I\}$. The formal analysis uses only D^j, without relying on the firms' strict preference relations.

The auction process is characterized by two functions, F and G. Define a function $G : \{\hat{w}_1, \ldots, \hat{w}_{N+1}\}^{I \times J} \to \{\hat{w}_0, \ldots, \hat{w}_{N+1}\}^{I \times J}$ as follows:

$$G_i^j(w) = \begin{cases} w_i^j \text{ if } i \in D^j(w^j) \\ p(w_i^j) \text{ otherwise} \end{cases}.$$

Suppose that w is the vector of wages that firms could offer to workers in the current round under the auction procedures. I argue next that $G_i^j(w)$ is the wage that firm j will actually offer to worker i in the current round.

Consider two cases. In the first case, worker i has rejected firm j's contract offer, and in that case, w_i^j is the next higher wage, and $p(w_i^j)$ is the wage the worker had rejected. If firm j still wants to hire worker i, even at the current higher wage, the condition $i \in D^j(w^j)$ will be satisfied, and the firm will offer wage $G_i^j(w) = w_i^j$. Otherwise, if the firm does not want to hire i at the higher wage, it will not increase its wage offer but will let it stand at $G_i^j(w) = p(w_i^j)$. Either way, $G_i^j(w)$ denotes the wage that firm j will offer to such a worker i in the current round. In the second case, worker i has not rejected j's previous wage offer, so (by gross substitutes) the condition $i \in D^j(w^j)$ is satisfied. Again, $G_i^j(w)$ is the wage the firm will offer. We include null offers in this formulation by allowing $G_i^j(w) = \hat{w}_0$ to describe the case in which j has made no offer to i.

The possible wages at each round of the auction are determined from those of the previous round by application of a function $F: \{\hat{w}_1, \ldots, \hat{w}_{N+1}\}^{I \times J} \rightarrow \{\hat{w}_1, \ldots, \hat{w}_{N+1}\}^{I \times J}$. This function incorporates both the firms' decisions and those of the workers. Given a wage vector w, each worker i considers his or her set of current contract offers and the possibility of unemployment: $\left\{\left(i, j, G_i^j(w)\right) \mid j \in J\right\} \cup \{\varnothing_i\}$. Based on his or her preferences, he or she rejects all but the best of these. Let $R_i(w) \subseteq \left\{j \mid i \in D^j(w^j)\right\}$ consist of firms that would demand worker i at the wage vector w^j

but that the worker would reject at those wages. Define $F:\{\hat{w}_1,\ldots,\hat{w}_{N+1}\}^{I\times J}\rightarrow\{\hat{w}_1,\ldots,\hat{w}_{N+1}\}^{I\times J}$ by:[4]

$$F_i^j(w)=\begin{cases} n(w_i^j) & \text{if } j\in R_i(w) \\ w_i^j & \text{if } j\notin R_i(w) \end{cases}.$$

Using F, the sequence of possible wage offers in the auction can be described as follows. Initialize $w_i^j(1)=\hat{w}_1$ for all i and j. Set $w(t+1)=F(w(t))$ (meaning that firms whose wage offers are rejected can consider making the next highest wage offer). Terminate the process at the earliest round T for which $w(T-1)=F(w(T-1))$ (when no firm will improve its offer to any worker). Thus, $w(T)=F^{T-1}(w(1))$.

When the auctions end, the final matching is $C=\{(i,j,w_i^j(T))\,|\,i\in D^j(w^j(T))\}\{\varnothing_i:\nexists\, j\in j:i\in D^j(w^j(T))\}$. These are exactly the contracts that are being offered by firms at wages in $w(T)$ and have never been rejected by the workers.

2.2.6 A CONNECTION TO CONTINUOUS COMPETITIVE EQUILIBRIUM

What is the connection between a stable augmented matching in this discrete model and a competitive equilibrium in the continuous model? In a competitive equilibrium (x,p), all agents maximize with respect to the prices p and the markets clear. In this discrete model, at prices $w(T)$, firms are maximizing, demanding exactly the workers that they want to hire. At the prices $G(w(T))$, workers are maximizing, each taking his or her best option. But in contrast to a competitive equilibrium, the prices considered by all agents are not the same: generally, $G(w(T)) < w(T)$.[5] Still, although the wages differ, these wages are as close together as possible: they are adjacent in the finite set of possible wages. So, if the model is formulated with small wage differences, then there is no significant economic difference between a stable augmented matching and a competitive equilibrium.

Given that similarity, are the auction processes similar as well? Let us now analyze some properties of the discrete dynamics more formally.

The first result is that the auction process does converge.

Proposition 2.2

The discrete auction process terminates in a finite number of rounds: $T < \infty$.

Proof

There are only finitely many different wages and $w(t+1) > w(t)$ in every round before the last. So, there can be only finitely many rounds. ■

Second, when workers are substitutes, firms always repeat at round $t+1$ any offer that was not rejected at round t. Our claim is outlined formally in proposition 2.3.

Proposition 2.3

Suppose workers are gross substitutes for the firm j. If $i \in D^j\left(w^j(t)\right)$ and $j \notin R_i(w)$, then $i \in D^j\left(w^j(t+1)\right)$.

Proof

Suppose that $i \in D^j\left(w^j(t)\right)$. By construction of the auction process, $w^j(t+1) \geq w^j(t)$. Since $j \notin R_i(w)$, it follows that $w_i^j(t+1) = w_i^j(t)$. Applying the definition of gross substitutes, $i \in D^j\left(w^j(t+1)\right)$. ■

This proposition is significant for two reasons. First, it has a subtle implication in the way we have specified the function *F*. Because the best previous offers will always be repeated in the actual auctions, we can construct *F* as if workers can choose to recall previous offers, without worrying that the offers that workers accept will be ones that the firms would want to withdraw. Second, this statement in the discrete model has roughly the same economic content as the statement in the continuous model that the prices always remain in the region where demand weakly exceeds supply for each good. The proposition implies that, in the discrete model, once there is any offer to a worker *i* at a wage that the worker prefers to being unemployed, the wage offer vector $w(t)$ always stays in a region where at least one firm *j* continues to demand that worker.

The last important economic conclusion, analogous to the continuous model, is that these auction processes converge up to the lowest wages associated with any stable matching.

Proposition 2.4

Assume that workers are gross substitutes for firms. Then, for any stable augmented matching, (w', C'), $w(T) \leq w'$.

The proof relies on the following lemma, which in turn relies on the gross substitutes condition and the construction of *F*.

Lemma 2.5

Assume that workers are gross substitutes for firms. Then, the function F is *isotone*: for any two wage profiles $w, w' \in W^{I\times J}$, if $w' \geq w$, then $F(w') \geq F(w)$.

The lemma is proved later. Here is how we use it to prove proposition 2.4.

Proof of Proposition 2.4

First, notice by construction of F that for any stable matching (w', C'), it must be true that $w' = F(w')$. Also, by the initial condition of the auction, $w(1) \leq w'$. Suppose that for some t, $w(t) \leq w'$. Then, since F is isotone, $w(t+1) = F(w(t)) \leq F(w') = w'$. So, $w(T) \leq w'$. ■

Proof of Lemma 2.5

Fix any worker $i \in I$ and firm $j \in J$. Since the domain and range of F are both the product of finite sets, it is sufficient to show that the component function $F_i^j(w)$ does not decrease when any component argument w_i^j is increased to its next value $n(w_i^j)$, with the other components held fixed. We denote that changed vector by $w \setminus n(w_i^j)$ and consider four exhaustive cases.

(i) Consider firm j increasing w_i^j. By construction, $F_i^j(w) \leq w_i^j \leq F_i^j\left(w \setminus n(w_i^j)\right)$.

(ii) Consider some firm $j' \neq j$ increasing $w_i^{j'}$. If $j \notin R_i(w)$, then $F_i^j(w) = w_i^j \leq F_i^j\left(w \setminus n(w_i^{j'})\right)$. If $j \in R_i(w)$, then $j \in R_i\left(w \setminus n(w_i^{j'})\right)$, so $F_i^j(w) = n(w_i^j) = F_i^j\left(w \setminus n(w_i^{j'})\right)$.

(iii) Consider firm j increasing $w_{i'}^j$ for some worker $i' \neq i$. By gross substitutes, if $i \in D^j(w)$ and $j \in R_i(w)$, then

$j \in R_i\left(w \setminus n(w_{i'}^j)\right)$, in which case $F_i^j(w) = F_i^j\left(w \setminus n(w_{i'}^j)\right)$. If $j \notin R_i(w)$, then $F_i^j(w) \leq w_i^j \leq F_i^j\left(w \setminus n(w_{i'}^j)\right)$.

(iv) Finally, consider firm $j' \neq j$ increasing $w_{i'}^{j'}$ for some worker $i' \neq i$. Then, always, $F_i^j(w) = F_i^j\left(w \setminus n(w_{i'}^{j'})\right)$. ■

There are four technical differences between the discrete and continuous models that led to changes in the analysis. First, instead of a continuous price process in continuous time, the analysis of the Kelso-Crawford model uses discrete prices and proceeds in discrete time. Second, the sellers (workers) do not choose the buyers (firms) based on price alone; they care about the identity of the firm as well. Third, since a worker's best opportunity cannot be identified by reference to just one wage, the algorithm needs to keep track of multiple wages for each worker. Our formulation here shows how to deal with the first three differences. Finally, firms and workers base their decisions on slightly different wages, whereas in competitive equilibrium, the same price vector is used by all parties. Despite these differences, the analysis and results in the two models are similar.

Here is a summary of our primary findings in this section about the discrete model when firms regard workers as gross substitutes:

- A stable augmented matching exists. For every stable augmented matching (w, C), firms hire the optimal set of workers as if they take the wage vector w as given, and workers choose the optimal jobs as if they assume that the available wages are given by the alternative wage vector $G(w)$, described as follows: if i is matched to j, then $G_i^j(w) = w_i^j$; otherwise, $G_i^j(w) = p(w_i^j)$.

- Among the wage vectors w that are part of some stable augmented matching (w, C), there is a lowest wage vector, that is, one in which each worker's wage is at least as low as in any other stable augmented matching. (There is also a highest one, not analyzed here.)
- Wage offers in an ascending auction, modeled as a discrete process in which firms bid for the workers they would most like to hire at the currently prevailing wages in the auction, converge monotonically upward to the lowest wage vector.

2.3 NEAR-SUBSTITUTES, PRICES, AND EFFICIENCY IN THE KNAPSACK PROBLEM

The previous sections treat prices in a way that is standard in economics—as associated with efficient and market-clearing outcomes. This can be very limiting, because in real-world auction design, goods are often discrete but not gross substitutes, and there is no guarantee that market-clearing prices exist. Indeed, Milgrom (2000) and Milgrom and Strulovici (2009) show that if the possible values for bidders in an auction include all additive preferences and also some preference that does not satisfy gross substitutes, then there are always instances in which market-clearing prices fail to exist.

Despite that limitation, auctions and the prices they generate can still be useful in finding nearly optimal resource allocations, particularly when goods are "near-substitutes." Recall that a set of goods in a particular model satisfies the substitutes condition if increasing the price of any one good never reduces the demand for any other good. When I say that the goods are *near-substitutes*, I mean that there is a nearby model in which some constraints are tightened or relaxed in which the goods are exactly substitutes. We will explore a suitable meaning for the term "nearby" later. The idea is most simply explored using the famous "knapsack problem," analyzed by Dantzig (1957).

2.3.1 KNAPSACK PROBLEMS AND A GREEDY ALGORITHM

Imagine that one has a container—a "knapsack"—and some discrete goods indexed by $n = 1, \ldots, N$. Each good n has an associated size s_n and value v_n. The knapsack problem is this: Select a set of goods to maximize the total value packed subject to the constraint that the total size of the items to be packed may not exceed the size S of the knapsack. To focus on just nontrivial problems, I assume that there is not enough space in the knapsack to pack everything, that is, $\Sigma_{n=1}^{N} s_n > S$.

The decisions to be made are described by variables x_n that indicate whether good n is to be included in the knapsack. Let $x_n = 1$ mean that the good is included and $x_n = 0$ mean that the good is not included. Then, $x = (x_1, \ldots, x_N) \in \{0, 1\}^N$ is a vector describing, for each good, whether it is packed in the knapsack. Let $v(x) \stackrel{\text{def}}{=} \Sigma_{n=1}^{N} v_n x_n$. The problem of packing the most valuable set of goods, and the corresponding optimal value $\bar{V}$, are described mathematically as follows:

$$\bar{V} = \max_{x \in \{0,1\}^N} v(x) \text{ subject to } \sum_{n=1}^{N} s_n x_n \leq S. \quad (1)$$

Suppose that a vector x is given and that it is claimed to be the optimal solution to (1). According to complexity theory, the problem of verifying that a proposed solution x of a knapsack problem is optimal is NP-complete, meaning roughly that it is very hard.[6] Roughly speaking, the reason it is so hard is that any algorithm may need to check, individually, a significant fraction of the combinations of N items to determine which ones might fit into the knapsack and whether that combination is more valuable than the proposed solution x. Because the number of combinations grows exponentially with the number of items N, when N is even moderately large, the solution time for any systematic algorithm can become impractically long.

Despite the difficulty of finding and checking an optimal solution, some practical progress can be made by studying a *relaxed* knapsack problem, in which we pretend that the goods are divisible. Here is a formal statement of the relaxed knapsack problem.

$$\bar{\bar{V}} = \max_{x \in [0,1]^N} v(x) \text{ subject to } \sum_{n=1}^{N} s_n x_n \leq S. \quad (2)$$

Mathematically, the difference between the original problem and the relaxed one is that in (1) the choice is a vector $x \in \{0,1\}^N$ (so every good must either be included or not), while in (2) the choice is a vector $x \in [0,1]^N$ (so goods can be fractionally included). The relaxed problem is a linear programming problem, and its optimal solution can be characterized using the following price:

$$\hat{p} = \inf\left\{ p \geq 0 \,\middle|\, \sum_{\{n \mid v_n > p s_n\}} s_n \leq S \right\}.$$

Any optimal solution of (2) is given as follows:

$$x_n = \begin{cases} 1 \text{ if } v_n > \hat{p} s_n \\ 0 \text{ if } v_n < \hat{p} s_n \end{cases}.$$

and, for any items n' (with $v_{n'} = \hat{p} s_{n'}$), set $x_{n'}$, so that $\Sigma_{n=1}^{N} s_n x_n = S$. If the solution to (2) is unique, then there is just one such good n' that is fractionally included in that solution. Even if there are multiple solutions, among them are some for which just one good is fractionally included.

The relaxed problem is an easy one. In fact, there is a monotonic algorithm to locate the optimal solution that processes the items one at a time without computing $\hat{p}$ in advance. It arranges the items in order according to the value/size ratio v_n/s_n, and processes them in order from highest to lowest. It packs each item until it encounters an item that does not fit in the remaining space. When such an item is encountered, the algorithm includes the fraction of that item that just fits in the knapsack, and then terminates. A moment's reflection will convince the reader that this algorithm does indeed pack optimally for the hypothetical case in which goods are divisible.

The key is that a similar algorithm can be applied heuristically to the actual, unrelaxed problem. It orders the goods in the same way as earlier, from highest value/size ratio v_n/s_n to the lowest such ratio. It then iteratively adds the unpacked item n until it encounters an item that cannot be fit into the remaining space in the knapsack. This is where the algorithm differs from the previous one. When an item does not fit, the algorithm sets the item aside and continues with the next item until all items have been processed.

This simple heuristic does not, in general, locate an optimal solution. For example, suppose there are two items and the knapsack has size $S=2$. The first item has size 1 and value 1.1; the second item has size 2 and value 2. The heuristic algorithm would begin by packing the first item (because $v_1/s_1=1.1$ and $v_2/s_2=1.0$). It would then find that there is no room remaining for the second item and terminate there, having found a solution with value 1.1. The optimal solution, however, is to pack item 2; that solution has value 2. Intuitively, the heuristic fails to find the optimal solution because it greedily adds items without regard to how the current choice may affect the ability to pack items that will be considered later. Heuristics of this sort are called "greedy algorithms."

In the general case, the proposed greedy algorithm works as follows. For each item $n=1,\dots,N$, compute the value per unit of size $p_n \overset{\text{def}}{=} v_n/s_n$. Renumber the items if necessary so that $p_1 \geq \dots \geq p_N$.[7] Starting with the first item $n=1$ and continuing in order, set $x_n=1$ if $s_n \leq S-\Sigma_{j=1}^{n-1} s_j x_j$ and otherwise set $x_n = 0$. This formalizes the idea described earlier that the heuristic considers the items in value/size order, packs each item if it still fits but otherwise sets it aside, and terminates when it has completed one pass through the list of items.

Define $S_m \stackrel{\text{def}}{=} S - \Sigma_{n=1}^{m-1} s_n$ and let $\hat{n}$ be the first item such that $\Sigma_{j=1}^{\hat{n}} s_j > S$. Recall that $\bar{V}$ denotes the optimal value of the knapsack problem. Since the solution to the relaxed problem provides an upper bound on the optimum, it must be true that $\bar{V} \leq \bar{\bar{V}} = \Sigma_{j=1}^{\hat{n}-1} v_j + p_{\hat{n}} S_{\hat{n}}$. We can use that inequality to bound the loss that can come from using the solution proposed by the greedy algorithm instead of using the optimal solution.

Proposition 2.6

Let V^{Greedy} denote the value achieved by the greedy solution and let $\bar{V}$ denote the optimal value. The difference between these two values is bounded by the following inequalities:

(i) $\bar{V} \geq V^{\text{Greedy}} \geq \bar{V} - p_{\hat{n}} S_{\hat{n}}$, and
(ii) for all $\hat{n} \in \mathbb{N}$, $(v_n, s_n)_{n=1}^{\hat{n}-1} \in \mathbb{R}_+^{2\hat{n}-2}$, and $\varepsilon > 0$, there exists $N \geq \hat{n}$ and $(v_n, s_n)_{n=\hat{n}}^{N} \in \mathbb{R}_+^{2(N+1-\hat{n})}$ such that $V^{\text{Greedy}} < \bar{V} - p_{\hat{n}} S_{\hat{n}} + \varepsilon$.

Point (ii) of the proposition means that the lower bound on V^{Greedy} given in part (i) is "tight"; adding any positive ε to that bound would make the general result false. The upper bound in (i) holds with equality when all items are of the same size, so it is also tight.

Proof of Proposition 2.6

For (i), the first inequality is obvious, and the second is proved in the preceding text.

For (ii), the case $S_{\hat{n}}=0$ is obvious, so let us assume that $(v_n,s_n)_{n=1}^{\hat{n}-1}$ are such that $S_{\hat{n}}>0$. We specify any $N\geq\hat{n}$ and $(v_n,s_n)_{n=\hat{n}}^{N}$ to satisfy $s_{\hat{n}}=S_{\hat{n}-1}>S_{\hat{n}}$, $p_{\hat{n}}=p_{\hat{n}-1}-\varepsilon/S_{\hat{n}-1}$, and $p_n=0$ for $n>\hat{n}$. In that case, $V^{\text{Greedy}}=\Sigma_{j=1}^{\hat{n}-1}v_j$. But it is feasible to pack items $1,\ldots,\hat{n}-2$ and item $\hat{n}$, so $\bar{V}>V^{\text{Greedy}}+p_{\hat{n}}S_{\hat{n}}-\varepsilon$. ■

In the relaxed problem, the goods are substitutes: increasing the value of any item n never increases the optimal choice of any x_m for $m\neq n$. In that sense, the actual knapsack problem captures the idea that goods are near-substitutes, but this near-substitutes condition is very different from the substitutes condition found in the previously studied discrete model of firms and workers. In the discrete model, if the firms are profit maximizers, then increasing a worker's wage to a firm could cause the firm to do one of two things: it might stop demanding that worker and make no other changes to its demand, or it might replace him or her by increasing its demand for exactly one other worker.[8] There are no other possibilities. One can express this by saying that the *rate of substitution* between workers in the discrete model is always either zero or one. In the relaxed knapsack model, there is no restriction on the rate of substitution among items. It can be optimal to substitute several small items for a big one in the knapsack, or one big one for several small ones. In the labor market setting, this corresponds to the idea that a firm might decide between hiring two half-time workers or one full-time worker. The labor market model did not incorporate that possibility, because such preferences for firms do not satisfy the substitutes restriction on which the analysis is based. Two part-time workers can be complements—not substitutes—because increasing the wage of one part-time worker can inspire a firm to withdraw its offer for another part-time worker and hire a full-time worker instead.

An important difference, then, between the discrete knapsack model and the discrete substitutes model treated earlier is that the knapsack model entails no restrictions on rates of substitution among items, either in the optimum or in the greedy solution.

To understand the mathematical ideas in this section and ones to follow, it is helpful to keep in mind that the substitutes property is a monotonicity property. Goods are substitutes when an increase in the price of one good raises the demand for another. The words "increase" and "raises" mean that we are appealing to an order property of demand, and to nothing else. What the mathematics reveals in this section and later ones is that this economic monotonicity is associated with the good performance of certain monotonic algorithms. The greedy algorithm has several monotonicity properties. An obvious one is that it adds to the set of items packed, without ever taking anything back. Soon, we will identify another of its monotonicity properties. Ascending auctions, too, are monotonic; they increase prices when there is excess demand without ever returning to reduce them again. Throughout this book, the propositions explaining that certain algorithms perform well when goods are substitutes, or nearly substitutes, all rely on certain exact or approximate monotonicity properties.

2.3.2 AN AUCTION BASED ON THE GREEDY ALGORITHM

To treat the knapsack problem as an auction problem, imagine that a different agent owns each different good. Each agent can enjoy the value of the good only if that agent acquires space for it in the knapsack. Assume that the size s_n of an item can be observed by both owner/bidder n and by the auctioneer, but that only the owner knows his or her own value, v_n, for the item.[9] We would like to show that there is some way to auction space in the knapsack so that the auction winners are the owners of the items that would be selected by the greedy algorithm if the vector of values v were known.

Let $\alpha_{\text{Greedy}}(v)$ denote the set of items that would be packed by the greedy algorithm when the values are given by the vector v. In general, any algorithm for the knapsack problem determines a function $\alpha(\cdot)$, so when the reported values are v, the items packed in the knapsack are those in the set $\alpha(v)$. With auctions in mind, we may also call this function the *winner selection rule*. To make it easy for bidders to choose their bids without having to guess about how others will bid, the auction should be "strategy-proof," which means roughly that each bidder should have the same best bid regardless of what he or she expects other bidders to do.

The key to the formal analysis is to recognize that the winner selection rule $\alpha_{\text{Greedy}}(v)$ has a particular monotonicity property, different from the one described earlier. This monotonicity property is that a winning bidder would remain a winner even if he or she were to increase his or her bid. That property implies that there exists some finite or infinite "threshold price" such that the bidder wins if he or she bids at least the threshold price and loses otherwise. If the auction rule specifies that any winning bidder must pay his or her threshold price, then the auction is called a "threshold auction." As we shall see, threshold auctions are always strategy-proof. Moreover, they are the *only* strategy-proof auctions.

Here is the corresponding formal development.

Definitions

1. A winner section rule $\alpha(v)$ is monotonic if $n \in \alpha(v)$ implies that for any $v_n' > v_n$, $n \in \alpha(v_n', v_{-n})$.
2. Given a monotonic winner selection rule α, the threshold price function is $\overline{v}_n^{\alpha}(v_{-n}) = \inf\{v_n \mid n \in \alpha(v_n, v_{-n})\}$.
3. A direct mechanism (α, p^{α}) is a *threshold auction* if the winner selection rule α is monotonic, each losing bidder pays zero, and each winning bidder n pays his or her threshold price $p_n^{\alpha}(v) = \overline{v}_n^{\alpha}(v_{-n})$.
4. A direct mechanism (α, p) is *strategy-proof* if for all profiles of values $v \in \mathbb{R}_+^N$ and every possible "false report" $v_n' \neq v_n$, the payoff to n from reporting v_n truthfully is at least as high as the payoff from reporting untruthfully:

$$(v_n - p_n(v))1_{n\in\alpha(v)} \geq (v_n - p_n(v_n', v_{-n}))1_{n\in\alpha(v_n', v_{-n})}.$$

For the greedy algorithm, an item n of value v_n is included in the knapsack if and only if there is still space for the item when its turn comes up during the processing. If the value of item n is increased to $v_n' > v_n$, then it comes up no later in the processing. Consequently, if the greedy algorithm includes item n when its value is v_n, it must also include the item when its value is v'_n. This argument implies that the winner selection rule α_{Greedy} is monotonic.

A particularly well-known example of a threshold auction is the famous second-price auction, which can be used to sell a single good. The winning bidder's threshold price in the second-price auction is the highest losing bid. The proof that the second-price auction is strategy-proof will be a familiar one to many readers. It can be routinely extended to establish the following result.

Proposition 2.7

For any monotonic winner selection rule, the corresponding threshold auction is strategy-proof.

Proof

We tabulate here the payoffs to a bidder who truthfully reports v_n or untruthfully reports v'_n, for various conditions on the reports and v_{-n}. In every case, truthful reporting

Condition	Payoff to report v_n	Comparison	Payoff to report v'_n
$\bar{v}_n^{\alpha}(v_{-n}) > max(v_n, v'_n)$	0	=	0
$\bar{v}_n^{\alpha}(v_{-n}) < \min(v_n, v'_n)$	$v_n - \bar{v}_n^{\alpha}(v_{-n})$	=	$v_n - \bar{v}_n^{\alpha}(v_{-n})$
$v_n \geq \bar{v}_n^{\alpha}(v_{-n}) \geq v'_n$	$v_n - \bar{v}_n^{\alpha}(v_{-n})$	≥	0
$v'_n \geq \bar{v}_n^{\alpha}(v_{-n}) \geq v_n$	0	≥	$v_n - \bar{v}_n^{\alpha}(v_{-n})$

pays at least as much as the false report, which proves the proposition. ■

In chapter 3 we will formulate and prove a proposition that implies a near converse to proposition 2.7. It asserts that for any monotonic winner selection rule α, and with the additional restrictions that (i) the set of possible values for each bidder n is an interval $[\underline{v}_n, \overline{v}_n]$, (ii) bidders have available the option to make a bid that always loses, and (iii) a losing bid always results in a zero payment, the threshold payment rule p^α is the unique one, such that (α, p^α) is strategy-proof. Moreover, for any winner selection rule α that is not monotonic, there is *no* pricing function p such that (α, p) is strategy-proof.[10]

Lehmann, O'Callaghan, and Shoham (2002) introduced a threshold auction based on the greedy winner selection rule α_{Greedy} and established that it is strategy-proof. As argued earlier, α_{Greedy} is monotonic, so their proposition follows from the previous one.

Proposition 2.8

The greedy winner selection rule α_{Greedy} is monotonic, and the associated "greedy threshold auction" is strategy-proof.

2.3.3 INVESTMENTS AND PSEUDO-EQUILIBRIUM

The usual analysis of the knapsack problem studies only which items are selected for packing. That can be an important problem, but individual resource-allocation problems can often be even more usefully conceived as part of a larger problem, in which other related resources must be allocated or other related decisions must be made. For packing problems, a common important decision concerns how much to invest in improving the items themselves, for example, making them smaller or more valuable, and in the capacity of knapsack, making it larger. The airspace example in the introduction illustrates the issues. In that example, decisions about the size and location of a new spaceport are sure to affect later decisions about commercial space launches, which in turn may disrupt other commercial uses. Setting proper prices helps to ensure that decision makers account for the costs their decisions will eventually have on other users and encourages the most profligate users to find ways to use fewer resources, for example, by finding good alternatives and/or simply curtailing the least valuable uses of resources.

In this section, I explore the extent to which prices in the knapsack problem can do double duty, serving not only to guide efficient packing of the knapsack but also to guide nearly efficient investments. My analysis can usefully be viewed through the lens of the first welfare theorem of neoclassical equilibrium theory, but replacing the assumption that markets clear exactly with an approximate market-clearing assumption. According to the first welfare theorem, if a vector of prices that leads price-taking decision makers to demand resources so that quantities supplied and demanded are exactly equal in all markets, then the decisions result in an efficient final allocation. In the approximate problem, there is an extra condition needed to ensure that prices that clear the markets approximately also provide reasonably good incentives for investment.

In the knapsack problem, the indivisibility of items typically prevents exact market clearing—some space is left vacant in the knapsack—so the older theory does not exactly apply. Nevertheless, it is not difficult to formalize the idea that the owners of individual items make decisions about the item sizes guided by an understanding of how much they expect to pay for space in the knapsack. Each owner chooses to shrink his or her item when the cost of doing so is less than the savings in the cost of space in the knapsack. In such a knapsack model, can the same price be used to guide both near-efficient investments and near-efficient packing in the knapsack?

The upshot of this discussion is that, besides strategy-proofness and approximate efficiency, another very desirable property of an auction mechanism for the knapsack problem is that it should produce a price of space that is a good guide to investments by the item owners. The simplest such mechanism would identify a price p^* that plays a role similar to that of a market-clearing price. This means that winning bidders are charged a price p^* per unit for space in the knapsack and that the winners are all the owners who are prepared to pay a price higher than p^*. In the general case, there will still be space left in the knapsack at that price, so p^* is not a market-clearing price. We call p^* a *pseudo-equilibrium price* (Milgrom and Strulovici, 2009) and compute it for any particular item values and sizes, using the following function:

$$P(v,s) \stackrel{\text{def}}{=} \inf\left\{ p \,\middle|\, \sum\nolimits_{\{n \mid v_n - ps_n > 0\}} s_n < S \right\}. \tag{3}$$

By construction, at prices lower than $p^* = P(v, s)$, there is excess demand for space in the knapsack. In the general case, in which there is no exact clearing price, there is strict excess supply at prices greater than p^*. If there is any exact clearing price for the problem, then p^* is one such price.

The same price p^* also has an interpretation that is relevant in the relaxed knapsack problem, where it corresponds to the marginal value of space in the knapsack. In contrast, for the ("discrete") knapsack problem, the marginal value of adding a small amount of space is always zero, so setting the price to the marginal value, which works well in case of exact market clearing, is not helpful to inform and guide efficient space-saving investments in the knapsack problem.

Verifying whether the levels of investment are efficient in the context of the knapsack problem is hard. Checking this may require solving multiple knapsack problems—corresponding to different patterns of investment—and that makes it at least as hard as verifying optimality in a single knapsack problem. What happens if we try to simplify by having the item owners act as price takers, with investments guided using the pseudo-equilibrium price p^*?

To study such questions, we introduce a new model—the *knapsack problem with investment*—in which each item owner n may be able to make an investment that affects the size and value of his or her item. An owner's choice opportunities are represented in the model by a finite set of triples $C_n \subseteq \mathbb{R}_+ \times \mathbb{R}_{++} \times \mathbb{R}_+$, where a choice $c_n = (v_n, s_n, i_n) \in C_n$ specifies that agent n will invest i_n to acquire a single item with value and size characteristics (v_n, s_n), where $s_n > 0$ and $(v_n, i_n) \geq 0$. The problem with investment also describes the size of the knapsack.

Definitions

1. A knapsack problem with investment is a $(N+1)$-tuple $\left(S,(C_n)_{n=1}^{N}\right)$ with $S>0$ and $C_n \subseteq \mathbb{R}_+ \times \mathbb{R}_{++} \times \mathbb{R}_+$.
2. A pseudo-equilibrium of the knapsack problem with investment $\left(S,(C_n)_{n=1}^{N}\right)$ is a pair $(p^*,c^*)=\left(p^*,(v_n^*,s_n^*,i_n^*,x_n^*)_{n=1}^{N}\right)$ satisfying two conditions:
   (i) $(v_n^*,s_n^*,i_n^*,x_n^*)$ solves $\max_{(v_n,s_n,i_n)\in C_n,\, x_n\in\{0,1\}} \left(v_n - p^* s_n\right)x_n - i_n$, and
   (ii) $p^* = P(v^*,s^*)$.

In the definition of pseudo-equilibrium, condition (i) says that owners choose optimally from their available choices, acting as if the price p^* is unaffected by their choices. The owners may be wrong in that assumption, because the price of space depends on their joint investment choices, as described by the function P. Condition (ii) describes that dependence. It says that the price of knapsack space is determined by a *short-run* pseudo–market clearing condition; the price is the "lowest" one at which the knapsack will not be filled or overfilled, given the existing investment decisions. Together, conditions i and ii imply that p^* is also, informally, a long-run pseudo–market clearing price, that is, the "long-run" choices c^* are also dependent on p^*.

Generally, the "long-run" demand for space by each owner is a nonincreasing step function of the market price of space. For generic choices of S, there is no price that supports exact market clearing, but there is always a unique pseudo-equilibrium price.

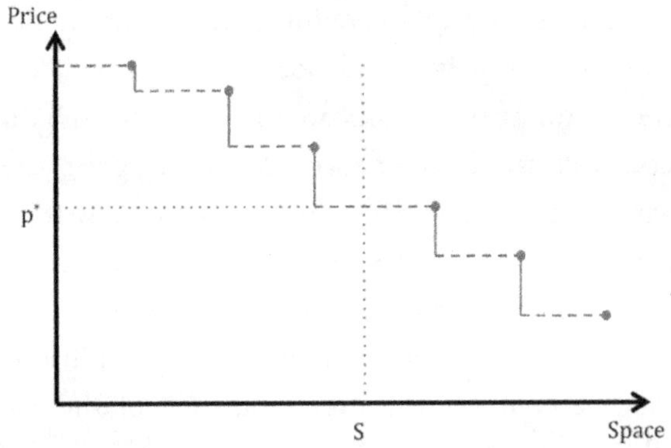

Figure 2.2 The long-run demand function for space in the knapsack, as a function of price, is a step function, represented by the solid vertical lines in the figure. For all sizes S of the knapsack, there is a unique pseudo-equilibrium price p^*, with the property that at higher prices, demand is less than or equal to supply, and at lower prices, demand strictly exceeds supply.

The space-reducing investments by owners in pseudo-equilibrium will not generally be efficient, and individual item owners can even make large errors in that respect. Here is an example to illustrate the point.

Example

There are two items, $N=2$. The total space in the knapsack is $S=2$. For the owner A of the first item, the possible choices are $C_A=\{a_1,a_2\}=\{(9,3,0),(2,1,1)\}$, and for the owner B of the second item, the possible choices are $C_B=\{b_1,b_2\}=\{(3,3,0),(3,1,1)\}$. At the optimal solution, both owners invest one to reduce their sizes, and both are packed into the knapsack.

In the unique pseudo-equilibrium of this model, the price of space is $p^* = 3$, and both owners find it optimal to invest zero. These choices are profit maximizing for the owners, given the price of space. Moreover, given the zero investments, neither item fits into the knapsack, so the short-run price formula specifies that the price must be three. In pseudo-equilibrium, the knapsack remains empty.

To assess the efficiency of the pseudo-equilibrium in general, we compare the total value V^* of the pseudo-equilibrium allocation to the optimal value $\bar{V}$ of the knapsack problem with investments. These two values are given by formulas (4) and (5):

$$V^* \stackrel{\text{def}}{=} \sum_{n=1}^{N} (v_n^* x_n^* - i_n^*) \tag{4}$$

and

$$\bar{V} \stackrel{\text{def}}{=} \max_{(v_n, s_n, i_n) \in C_n, x_n \in \{0,1\},} \sum_{n=1}^{N} (v_n x_n - i_n)$$

$$\text{subject to} \sum_{n=1}^{N} x_n s_n \leq S. \tag{5}$$

Proposition 2.9

Let $\left(p^*, (v_n^*, s_n^*, i_n^*, x_n^*)_{n=1}^N\right)$ be a pseudo-equilibrium and let $\bar{V}$ be defined as in (5). Then, $\bar{V} \geq V^* \geq \bar{V} - p^*(S - \Sigma_{\{n|v_n^* - p^* s_n^* > 0\}} s_n^*)$.

We interpret $p^*(S - \Sigma_{\{n|v_n^* - p^* s_n^* > 0\}} s_n^*)$ as the value of the empty space in the knapsack, with "value" computed using the pseudo-equilibrium price. Proposition 2.9 says that this value is an upper bound for the difference between the optimal value and the value of the items packed in a pseudo-equilibrium.

Proof of Proposition 2.9

Consider the variation of problem (5), in which we first add the term $p^*(S-\Sigma_{n=1}^{N} s_n x_n)$ to the objective—that term is nonnegative on the feasible set—and, second, eliminate the knapsack constraint. The value of this alternative problem is:

$$\bar{\bar{V}} = \max_{(v_n, s_n, i_n)\in C_n,\, x_n\in\{0,1\}} \sum_{n=1}^{N} \left(x_n(v_n - p^* s_n) - i_n\right) + p^* S \quad (6)$$

$$= p^* S + \sum_{n=1}^{N} \max_{(v_n, s_n, i_n)\in C_n,\, x_n\in[0,1]} \left(x_n(v_n - p^* s_n) - i_n\right)$$

$$= V^* + p^*\left(S - \sum_{\{n|v_n^* - p^* s_n^* > 0\}} s_n^*\right).$$

The two changes made to (5) to derive (6) can each only increase the maximum value, so, $\bar{V} \le \bar{\bar{V}} = V^* + p^*(S - \Sigma_{n=1}^{N} s_n^* x_n^*)$. ■

The pseudo-equilibrium price formula takes the values v_n^* and sizes s_n^* as given, but these are the results of forward-looking investment choices that take prices as given. In the pseudo-equilibrium, any owner whose item n will not be included in the knapsack does not invest (chooses the minimum level of i_n), which determines a size and value, and chooses $x_n = 0$.

Proposition 2.9 provides an interesting bound on the inefficiency of pseudo-equilibrium. We had previously found that the worst-case loss from inefficient packing in the simple knapsack problem can be tightly bounded by the product of a similarly computed equilibrium price and the empty space in the knapsack. In the knapsack problem *with investment*, things would seem to be worse, because losses can arise in two ways: inefficient packing and inefficient investment choices. Our earlier example does show that investment decisions can be poor. Nevertheless, according to proposition 2.9, the bound on the total worst-case loss from both inefficiencies still has the same product form. Whether this identifies "reasonably good" investment incentives is a matter of interpretation, in which examples as well as theorems play a useful role.

2.3.4 A UNIFORM-PRICE AUCTION FOR SPACE IN THE KNAPSACK

The pseudo-equilibrium structure is very simple, but it does not tell us how the price is to be discovered. Our goal is to find that price using a strategy-proof direct mechanism based on a variation of the greedy algorithm. We will call this variation the "truncated greedy algorithm," because it tracks the greedy algorithm but ends earlier and consequently packs just a subset of the items that are packed by a standard greedy algorithm.

Thus, define the winner selection rule α_{Trunc} by adding an early-termination condition to the standard greedy algorithm. For each round before termination, the truncated algorithm operates just the same as the greedy algorithm, but it stops processing items when it first encounters an item $\hat{n}$ such that $\Sigma_{j=1}^{\hat{n}} s_j > S$. Thus, the items it packs are given by $\alpha_{\text{Trunc}}(v,s)=\{1,\ldots,\hat{n}-1\}$, or equivalently, $\alpha_{\text{Trunc}}(v,s)=\{n \mid p_n > P(v,s)\}$. This is the same set of items packed in the pseudo-equilibrium. Also, by construction, $P(v,s)=p_{\hat{n}}$.

Although the truncated greedy algorithm never packs any items that would be excluded by the standard greedy algorithm, its worst-case performance bound is similar.

Proposition 2.10

Let $V^{\text{Trunc}}=\Sigma_{j=1}^{\hat{n}-1}v_j$ denote the total value of the set of items packed by the truncated greedy algorithm. Then, $\bar{V}\geq V^{\text{Trunc}}\geq\bar{V}-P(v,s)S_{\hat{n}}$. The lower bound is also *tight*, that is, for all $(v_n,s_n)_{n=1}^{\hat{n}-1}$, for every $\varepsilon>0$, there exists N and $(v_n,s_n)_{n=\hat{n}}^{N}\in\mathbb{R}_{+}^{N+1-\hat{n}}\times\mathbb{R}_{++}^{N+1-\hat{n}}$ such that $V^{\text{Trunc}}\leq\bar{V}-P(v,s)S_{\hat{n}}+\varepsilon$.

The proof is essentially just the same as the proof of proposition 2.6.

Another appeal of this winner selection rule is that its threshold prices mimic those of the pseudo-equilibrium.

Proposition 2.11

The winner selection rule α_{Trunc} associated with the truncated greedy algorithm is monotonic. Its corresponding threshold auction sets the price of any winner n to $P(v,s)s_n$. This *truncated greedy threshold auction* is strategy-proof.

Proof

By construction, $n\in\alpha_{\text{Trunc}}(v,s)$ if and only if $v_n/s_n>P(v,s)$, which proves both that α_{Trunc} is monotonic and that n's threshold price is $P(v,s)s_n$. The third statement follows from proposition 2.7. ■

Thus, in the special case without investment choices, the truncated greedy threshold auction computes both the pseudo-equilibrium allocation and pseudo-equilibrium prices for the participants.

2.3.5 NASH EQUILIBRIUM INVESTMENTS

So far, we have studied the choice of investment only in pseudo-equilibrium, in which owners are assumed to act as price takers. A partial justification for this is that no owner can, by manipulating its value report, alter the threshold price it must pay to be packed. However, owners can influence the price of space through their own investments. The $P(v, s)$ function captures that very influence.

The standard economic paradigm suggests that we formulate the knapsack problem not as a problem of selecting which items to pack, but in a subtly different way, as a problem of deciding how much space to allocate to each bidder. From this perspective, the item owners are simply purchasers of a homogeneous commodity—space in the knapsack—that is offered at some particular price.

As is usual in markets with few buyers, buyers have an incentive to artificially reduce their demand for space in order to reduce the price of space compared with the pseudo-equilibrium price. There are, however, two catches to this reasoning. The first catch arises from the fact that each owner has just an individual item to pack. An owner who withholds demand can reduce the price but then cannot benefit from the lower price. That objection still leaves open the possibility that the owner might benefit from making a space-reducing investment. We might therefore expect buyers to be tempted to make larger than optimal investments in saving space.

The second catch is that the pseudo-equilibrium price is set by an unsuccessful buyer, and such a buyer has no incentive to invest in the quality or value of his or her item, even if he or she would be called upon to invest at the allocation that maximizes total value. These caveats add subtlety to the formal statements.

To study the investment question mathematically, I will use a game-theoretic formulation. For readers who are unfamiliar or rusty with game theory, here is a digression to recount the game-theoretic concepts I will use.

Game Theory Digression

Definition

A *game* (*in strategic form*) is a triple $\Gamma = \left(\mathcal{N}, (\mathcal{S}_n)_{n\in\mathcal{N}}, (\pi_n)_{n\in\mathcal{N}} \right)$, where $\mathcal{N}$ is the set of players, $\mathcal{S}_n$ is the set of strategies available to player n, and $\pi_n : \times_{j\in\mathcal{N}} \mathcal{S}_j \to \mathbb{R}$ is the payoff function for player n, which specifies its payoff as a function of the profile of strategies played by all the players.

In some games, there may be an obvious strategy for a bidder to play, roughly because the strategy does better for the player than any other strategy, regardless of what strategies the other players may choose. Such a strategy is said to be "dominant." The formal definition of dominance is a bit more nuanced, allowing that sometimes a dominant strategy is only just as good as the alternative, as long as it is never worse and is sometimes better.

Definition

A strategy $s_n \in \mathcal{S}_n$ is *dominant* for player n if, for every other strategy $\hat{s}_n \in \mathcal{S}_n$, two conditions are satisfied: (1) for every profile of other players' strategies $s_{-n} \in \mathcal{S}_{-n}$, $\pi_n(s_n, s_{-n}) \geq \pi_n(\hat{s}_n, s_{-n})$, and (2) for some profile of other players' strategies $\hat{s}_{-n} \in \mathcal{S}_{-n}$, $\pi_n(s_n, \hat{s}_{-n}) > \pi_n(\hat{s}_n, \hat{s}_{-n})$.

This definition is closely connected to that of strategy-proof mechanisms, which were just treated previously. A mechanism is strategy-proof if, in the associated games (created by varying the players' values), truthful reporting is always a dominant strategy.

For strategic form games, the most famous solution is the one proposed by John Nash (1950).

Definition

Given a game $\Gamma = (\mathcal{N}, (\mathcal{S}_n)_{n \in \mathcal{N}}, (\pi_n)_{n \in \mathcal{N}})$, a strategy profile $s^* \in \times_{j \in \mathcal{N}} \mathcal{S}_j$ is a *pure Nash equilibrium* if, for every player $n \in \mathcal{N}$, $s_n^* \in argmax_{s_n \in \mathcal{S}_n} \pi_n(s_n, s_{-n}^*)$.[11]

When a strategy profile s^* is a pure Nash equilibrium, each player's strategy is the best choice he or she can make to maximize his or her own payoff, given that the other players are playing their equilibrium strategies, too. The interpretations of Nash equilibrium in practice, and when it is likely to be a good description of behavior, have received enormous attention from game theorists. Readers who are new to game theory are warned that this area is controversial, and it is surely not true that Nash equilibrium play is always to be expected or that every Nash equilibrium is equally likely. The discussion of those questions is beyond the scope of this book.

Back to the Investment Game

In the game model, the players are the owners of the items in the knapsack problem. Notice that after those players have made their investments and the time arrives to report values, the remainder of the mechanism is strategy-proof: truthful reporting is a dominant strategy for all players. To focus the formal analysis on investment incentives, I formulate the game without the value-reporting move by just assuming that each player will report truthfully, treating investments as the only strategic decisions.

Formally, the game is one in which the players are the owners and a strategy for owner n is $c_n = (v_n, s_n, i_n) \in C_n$. Let $c \stackrel{\text{def}}{=} (c_1, \ldots, c_N)$. An owner's payoff is

$$\pi_n(c) = \left(v_n - P(v,s)s_n\right)1_{\{v_n > P(c)s_n\}} - i_n.$$

In this game formulation, our main finding is that the simple economic intuition described earlier gives an incomplete account for this problem: it misses the possibility that there may exist multiple Nash equilibria, that is, multiple strategy profiles that are all Nash equilibria. Some of these may involve a failure of bidders to coordinate on some mutually beneficial outcome. Here is an example to illustrate that.

Example

There are two items, $N = 2$. The total space in the knapsack is $S = 2$. For owner A of the first item, the possible choices are $C_A = \{a_1, a_2\} = \{(12, 3, 0), (2, 1, 1)\}$, and for owner B of the second item, the possible choices are $C_B = \{b_1, b_2\} = \{(9,3,0),(3,1,1)\}$.

There are two pure Nash equilibria in this game: (a_1, b_1) and (a_2, b_2). In the first equilibrium, both item owners make investments of zero and have items that are too large for the knapsack. Nothing is packed in equilibrium. Owner B has no profitable unilateral deviation because it cannot be packed when A is not and it cannot beat A's value/size ratio of four. Owner A could invest one to make its item smaller (and less valuable), but then B would come first in the truncated greedy algorithm, ending the matter, because B's item does not fit.

In the second Nash equilibrium, both item owners make investments of one and both fit into the knapsack. In this equilibrium, each pays a price of zero for the space that he or she receives.

The existence theorem for Nash equilibrium (Nash, 1950; or for a modern textbook treatment, Fudenberg and Tirole, 1991) promises only that every finite-player, finite-strategy game has at least one mixed equilibrium, but the proposition offered later limits attention to pure Nash equilibrium.

Assume that, as in figure 2.2, the pseudo-equilibrium does not exactly fill the knapsack. In a Nash equilibrium, unlike in pseudo-equilibrium, each owner/player in the game accounts for the fact that his or her investment choices may influence the price that he or she must pay for space in the knapsack. The return to such investments is enjoyed only for items that win a space in the knapsack, so a loser n makes no investment. That is, he or she makes the choice c_n with the lowest value of i_n.

Recall that, according to the law of demand, demand curves slope downward. This means that when a price increases, buyers demand less of the good in question.[12] A consequence is that when we begin with a pseudo-equilibrium and one participant's demand for space is increased, the new pseudo-equilibrium price must rise, at least weakly, to elicit offsetting reductions in the quantities demanded by other participants. Therefore, if a winning bidder reduces the size of his or her item, demanding less space, the pseudo-equilibrium price must fall (weakly). Formally, for any c_n and c_n' such that n is a winner and $s_n < s_n'$, the conclusion is that $P(c_n, c_{-n}^*) \leq P(c_n', c_{-n}^*)$.

These facts lead to the following additional conclusion.

Proposition 2.12

For any knapsack problem with investments $\left(S, (C_n)_{n=1}^N\right)$, let $\hat{c}$ be a pure Nash equilibrium of the truncated greedy auction mechanism and let c^* denote the corresponding pseudo-equilibrium choices. Then, (i) $P(\hat{c}) \leq P(c^*)$ and (ii) $v_n^* > P(c^*)s_n^* \Rightarrow \hat{v}_n > P(\hat{c})\hat{s}_n$. (The price is weakly lower in the Nash equilibrium, and every item that is packed in the pseudo-equilibrium is also packed in the Nash equilibrium.)

Proof

First, assume to the contrary of (i) that $P(\hat{c}) > P(c^*)$. We will argue that $P(\hat{c})$ must be a pseudo-equilibrium price, violating the uniqueness of pseudo-equilibrium prices.

Denote n's price-taking profit by π_n, and let $\bar{c}$ describe the optimum individual choices, taking $P(\hat{c})$ as given. Take any Nash equilibrium winner $w \in \hat{W}$, $\pi_w\left(\hat{c}_w, P(\hat{c})\right) \geq 0 \Rightarrow$

$\pi_w\left(\hat{c}_w, P(c^*)\right) > 0$. Hence, each $w \in \hat{\mathcal{W}}$ must demand a positive amount of space in the pseudo-equilibrium $P(c^*)$. And by the law of demand, $P(\hat{c}) > P(c^*) \Rightarrow \bar{s}_w \leq s^*_w$, which implies that $\Sigma_{w \in \hat{\mathcal{W}}} \bar{s}_w \leq \Sigma_{w \in \hat{\mathcal{W}}} s^*_w \leq S$. So, using $\bar{c}_w$ for $w \in \hat{\mathcal{W}}$, the winner's nonnegative demand still fits in S.

Second, as explained earlier (by the internalization of investment decisions), $\bar{s}_n \geq \hat{s}_n$ for every player. Thus, for each Nash equilibrium loser $l \in \hat{\mathcal{L}}$, $\bar{s}_l$ will still fail to fit in S. So, $\bar{c}_l$ is still a losing allocation, and for all $l \in \hat{\mathcal{L}}$, $\bar{\imath}_l = \hat{\imath}_l = \min\{i_l : c_l \in C_l\}$ and $\pi_l\left(\bar{c}_l, P(\hat{c})\right) = -\bar{\imath}_l$. Then, the optimum profile $\bar{c}$ is a feasible allocation for every player, taking $P(\hat{c})$ as given.

We are only left to prove that $P(\hat{c})$ is the infimal price supporting $\bar{c}$. Take any price P' lower than $P(\hat{c})$. By construction of $P(\hat{c})$, there existed at least one $\tilde{l} \in \hat{\mathcal{L}}$, such that $\hat{v}_{\tilde{l}} - P'\hat{s}_{\tilde{l}} > 0$, implying $\pi_l\left(\hat{c}_l, P'\right) > -\hat{\imath}_l = -\bar{\imath}_l$, a profitable deviation by $\tilde{l}$ that will induce excess demand. Then, $P(\hat{c})$ is the pseudo-equilibrium price, which is a contradiction. We may conclude that $P(\hat{c}) \leq P(c^*)$. Part (ii) is then obvious by using (i) and the law of demand. ■

In intuitive terms, our key findings about the knapsack problem are these:

- Knapsack problems entail a kind of approximate substitution, as different items compete for space in the knapsack. Because items may differ in size, the rates of substitution among items are unrestricted—for example, one may be able to replace one large item in the knapsack with two smaller ones. That contrasts with the Kelso-Crawford model, in which adding one worker leads the firm to replace either zero or one other worker.

- Knapsack problems are computationally challenging, an NP-hard class of problems.
- For a large set of knapsack problems, however, a simple greedy algorithm can often locate a solution that reasonably approximates the optimum and comes with a useful bound on the maximum loss that the solution entails.
- The greedy algorithm has an associated strategy-proof auction, known as the "greedy threshold auction."
- An extension of the knapsack problem, called the "knapsack problem with investment," studies the incentives of item owners to invest in making their items smaller or more valuable.
- A *pseudo-equilibrium*, which sets the unique price such that the knapsack is overfilled at higher prices and underfilled at lower prices, provides an analogy to equilibrium models for the case when space is divisible.
- In the knapsack problem with investment, the pseudo-equilibrium outcome provides a bound on the loss that takes the same form as the bound in the model without investment, suggesting that the loss of value from poor investment incentives may be low. Pseudo-equilibrium, however, assumes price-taking behavior by the item owners.
- The pseudo-equilibrium price and allocation can be computed by the "truncated greedy algorithm," which is a strategy-proof direct auction mechanism.
- The investments that result from the truncated greedy auction lead to weakly lower prices than pseudo-equilibrium.

2.4 ASSIGNMENT CONSTRAINTS AND ONE-FOR-ONE SUBSTITUTES

In this section, we again study a problem of a single auctioneer and many bidders: in this case, a single buyer and multiple sellers. There are two key differences between the model in this section and the preceding one. First, there can be many constraints on the auctioneer, rather than just the single knapsack constraint. Second, as in the Kelso-Crawford model, the local rates of substitution implied by the constraints are always zero or one. This means that given a set of items S to which we wish to add one more item n, if space can be made for that item by removing a subset of items $T \subseteq S$, then there is some $m \in T$ such that space can be made by removing just the one item m. In a knapsack setting, this would correspond to the case in which all items are the same size.

To illustrate the main ideas, think about a case in which a firm needs to hire a sufficient team of workers to do a job or the government needs to acquire a sufficient set of TV stations to clear the spectrum for its planned alternative uses. For simplicity, assume that the buyer's objective is to minimize the cost of acquiring a sufficient set of items to meet its needs.[13] In our abstract model, there is no need to distinguish between a seller and the good it supplies, so both will be denoted by n. Seller n's value for its good is denoted v_n, where $0 < v_n < \overline{v}$. We let $\mathcal{A}$ denote the set of acceptable collections of goods, meaning that a set of goods S is acceptable if and only if $S \in \mathcal{A}$. The buyer's goal is to identify the least expensive set of items to acquire while satisfying its constraints.

So far, this formulation incorporates the knapsack problem as a special case, but with a twist compared with the previous section. If the goods in this formulation had various sizes and if an acceptable set $S \in \mathcal{A}$ is one that achieves at least a particular total size (or, equivalently, its complement S^C is at most some total size), then the problem of selecting *losers* would be a knapsack problem. One could find an approximate optimum for that problem by using the previously described greedy algorithm.

In this section, we allow multiple constraints, which are given in terms of the set of goods the buyer does *not* acquire. For example, in the incentive auction, in order to reassign frequencies to wireless broadband uses, the government needs to assign channels to the stations that it does not acquire and hence will continue to broadcast television signals. Furthermore, the channel assignment must be arranged so that the signals do not interfere with one another. This potentially involves a large number of separate constraints. For example, separate constraints limit the number of TV stations assigned to channels in New York City and Boston. In addition, if broadcasts from both Boston and New York City interfere with stations located in between, say in Connecticut, there may also be an overall limit on the number of stations that remain in the two cities combined.[14]

Given any set of goods $S \subseteq \mathcal{N} = \{1, \ldots, N\}$, let S^C denote its complement. Recall that $\mathcal{A}$ represents the collection of sets of goods that the buyer can feasibly accept, so $\mathcal{R} = \{S \mid S^C \in \mathcal{A}\}$ consists of the collections of goods that the buyer can feasibly reject. The problem is to minimize the total cost (value) of the set of stations A that are acquired or, equivalently, to maximize the total value (cost) of the set of stations R that are *not* acquired. Defining $v(R) \stackrel{\text{def}}{=} \Sigma_{n \in R} v_n$, we formulate the problem as follows:

$$\max_{R \in \mathcal{R}} v(R). \tag{7}$$

In this section, we analyze cases in which the buyer needs to acquire at least a certain set of goods and those goods are *one-for-one substitutes*. This means that the collection $\mathcal{R}$ has these mathematical properties:

(1) Feasibility: $\varnothing \in \mathcal{R}$.
(2) Free disposal: for any set $S \in \mathcal{R}$ and any subset $S' \subset S$, it must be that $S' \in \mathcal{R}$.
(3) Augmentation property (one-for-one substitution): given $S, S' \in \mathcal{R}$, if $|S| > |S'|$, then there exists $n \in S - S'$ such that $S' \cup \{n\} \in \mathcal{R}$.

In mathematics, a collection $\mathcal{R}$ with properties (1)–(3) is called a *matroid*.[15] In economic terms, property 1 says that the problem is feasible: there is some way for the buyer to meet its needs (for example, accepting everything and rejecting nothing). Property 2 says that it never hurts the buyer to have extra items, that is, if the buyer can meet its needs by rejecting the items in S and acquiring those in S^C, then it can also do so by rejecting the smaller set S' and acquiring the larger set S'^C. Property 3 corresponds to the economic idea of one-for-one substitution: all maximal independent subsets of any set S have the same number of elements. If we had formulated the knapsack problem in a similar way, specifying that $\mathcal{R}$ consists of sets of goods that could be fit into a knapsack, then such a condition would not generally be satisfied. A knapsack might, in general, be completely filled by one large item or several smaller items.

Examples

1. Suppose that $N = 15$, that the buyer needs to acquire at least ten items, and that any ten items will do. Then, $\mathcal{R}$ consists of all subsets of $\mathcal{N}$ with no more than five items. Let us check properties 1–3 for this example.
   a. $\mathcal{R}$ includes the empty set ($\varnothing \in \mathcal{R}$).
   b. If $S \in \mathcal{R}$, then S has at most five elements, so any subset $S' \subset S$ has at most four elements, and $S' \in \mathcal{R}$.
   c. If $|S| > |S'|$, then (i) S' has strictly fewer than five elements, and (ii) there is some element $n \in S - S'$, so S' can be augmented by adding n while still having no more than five elements.
2. Suppose the buyer needs to acquire at least ten items from a set with $N = 15$ items, but at least two of the items must be colored blue and three must be colored red, where the color is a fixed attribute of each item. Suppose that $\mathcal{N}$ contains $b \geq 2$ blue items and $r \geq 3$ red items. Then, $\mathcal{R}$ consists of all subsets of $\mathcal{N}$ with no more than five items, among which at most $b-2$ are blue and at most $r-3$ are red.
   a. $\mathcal{R}$ includes the empty set.
   b. If $S \in \mathcal{R}$ has no more than five items and no more than $b-2$ blue items and $r-3$ red items, then any subset $S' \subset S$ has those same properties, so $S' \in \mathcal{R}$.

c. For the augmentation property, suppose that $S, S' \in \mathcal{R}$ and $|S| > |S'|$. Compared with S', the set S contains either (i) more blue items or (ii) more red items or (iii) more items that are neither blue nor red. S' can be augmented in case (i) by adding some blue item from S, in case (ii) by adding some red item from S, and in case (iii) by adding some item from S that is neither blue nor red while still satisfying all of the constraints.

3. Suppose a sports team has K *positions*, labeled $\{1, \ldots, K\}$ and must hire a player for each. The potential hires are labeled $\{1, \ldots, N\}$, and each player n has a set of positions P_n that he or she is able to play. A set of players $S \subseteq \{1, \ldots, N\}$ is *feasible to accept* if, for every position k, there exists an assignment of positions to players $\alpha : S \to \{1, \ldots, K\}$, such that $\alpha(n) = k$ implies $k \in P_n$. A set R is feasible to reject if it is feasible to accept the complementary set. Let us assume that it is feasible to accept the full set of players $\{1, \ldots, N\}$.

   a. $\mathcal{R}$ includes the empty set.

   b. Suppose that $R \in \mathcal{R}$ and $R' \subseteq R$. Then $S = \{1, \ldots, N\} - R$ can be accepted and has an associated feasible assignment function α. Let $S' = \{1, \ldots, N\} - R'$. Then, $S \subseteq S'$, so any function α' whose restriction to S coincides with α works as an assignment for S'. Hence, $R' \in \mathcal{R}$.

   c. To prove the augmentation property, suppose that $R, \hat{R} \in \mathcal{R}$ and $|R| > |\hat{R}|$. Let S and $\hat{S}$ be the complements of R and $\hat{R}$, respectively, with assignment functions α and $\hat{\alpha}$. Since $|S| < |\hat{S}|$, there is some position k such that $\left|\hat{\alpha}^{-1}(k)\right|>\left|\alpha^{-1}(k)\right|\geq 1$. Let n be any element of $\hat{S}-S$ such that $\alpha(n)=k$. Then, we can augment $\hat{R}$ by adding the element $n\in R$.

The three properties described characterize not only a particular economic allocation problem in which goods are *substitutes*, but also the famous *matroid* structure from combinatorial mathematics. This structure arises repeatedly in many different kinds of applications. How the standard mathematical terms correspond to those of our economic application is explained in the following section.

Matroid Theory Terminology

- The set $\mathcal{N}$ of potentially available items is called the *ground set*.
- The sets in $\mathcal{R}$ of potentially rejected sets of items are called *independent sets*.
- The collection of independent sets $\mathcal{R}$ is a *matroid* if and only if it has properties 1–3.
- S is a *basis* of $\mathcal{R}$ if it is a maximal element of $\mathcal{R}$, that is, if $S\in\mathcal{R}$ and for all $S'\subseteq\mathcal{N}$, $[S\subset S']\Rightarrow[S'\notin\mathcal{R}]$.

It is easy to see from the augmentation property that all the bases of $\mathcal{R}$ have the same number of elements, a property that we rely upon later.

Matroids are significant for this analysis because of the way greedy algorithms perform when the constraints form a matroid. Later, we describe a greedy algorithm to sort goods between those that are to be accepted or rejected.

The two resulting sets are denoted by A ("accepted") and R ("rejected"). Along the way, the partially constructed sets at iteration n are denoted by R_n and A_n, respectively.

Greedy Rejection Algorithm

Arrange the indices so that $v_1 \geq \ldots \geq v_N$.

1. Set $R_0 = A_0 = \varnothing$ and $n=0$.
2. Increment n by 1.
3. If $n = N+1$, stop and output $R = R_N$ and $A = A_N$.
4. If $R_{n-1} \cup \{n\} \in \mathcal{R}$, set $R_n = R_{n-1} \cup \{n\}$ and $A_n = A_{n-1}$; if $R_{n-1} \cup \{n\} \notin \mathcal{R}$, set $R_n = R_{n-1}$ and $A_n = A_{n-1} \cup \{n\}$.
5. Go to step 2.

Example

In the sports team described earlier, let $K = 2$ and $N = 4$ represent the positions and potential hires such that $P_1 = P_2 = \{1\}$, $P_3 = P_4 = \{2\}$ and $v_1 = 3, v_2 = 2, v_3 = 1, v_4 = 0$. The potentially rejected sets are $\mathcal{R} = \{\{1\}, \{2\}, \{3\}, \{4\}, \{1,3\}, \{1,4\}, \{2,3\}, \{2,4\}\}$.

In the first round, the greedy rejection algorithm sets $R_1 = \{1\}$, $A_1 = \varnothing$. In the second round, the algorithm will fail to reject player 2, setting $R_2 = \{1\}, A_2 = \{2\}$. After four rounds, the final allocation will be $R = \{1,3\}, A = \{2,4\}$.

Intuitively, the algorithm sorts items by a series of steps at which it always evaluates the most costly remaining item, rejecting it if rejection is feasible, otherwise accepting it. For example, if the feasible sets to reject are ones with no more than K items in total, then the greedy algorithm rejects the K most costly items and accepts the remaining items, which are the cheapest ones.

The problem that we are studying is not generally a knapsack problem, because the constraints are specified differently and the procedure is greedy rejection, rather than greedy inclusion. Nevertheless, nearly the same argument that we employed earlier applies, and it again implies that the greedy algorithm is monotonic. In this case, the argument is that reducing the value of an item makes it come up for consideration later, and it is then less likely to be rejected. By proposition 2.7, that implies the following:

Proposition 2.13

The winner selection rule for the greedy rejection algorithm described earlier is monotonic. The corresponding threshold auction is strategy-proof.

We highlight two additional properties as well. The first concerns the performance of the greedy algorithm for this set of problems.

Proposition 2.14

If $\mathcal{R}$ is a matroid, then the output R of a greedy rejection algorithm is an optimal solution to (7).

The proof is by induction, but an easy intuition can be acquired by thinking about just the first choice of the greedy algorithm. Why is it okay to take the most valuable item? Might that not block future valuable choices? The answer lies in the augmentation property. For suppose that some set S

of k items does not include the most valuable item. By the augmentation property, we can then repeatedly select items from S to combine with the most valuable item to create a set S' of k items that differs from S in just one item. By construction, the one additional item in S' is the most valuable item, so the value of S' is higher than the value of S. Hence, the optimal set must include the most valuable item.

Proof of Proposition 2.14

Suppose to the contrary that the greedy solution $R=\{r_1,\ldots,r_k\}$ is not optimal and that instead S is an optimal solution. Let $n=\min\{j|r_j\notin S\}$. By repeated application of the augmentation property, there is some $S'\subset S-\{r_1,\ldots,r_{n-1}\}$ such that $S''\stackrel{\text{def}}{=}\{r_1,\ldots,r_n\}\cup S'\in\mathcal{R}$. Thus, for some $\hat{s}\in S'$, $S''=S\cup\{r_n\}-\{\hat{s}\}$. But then S cannot be optimal, because $\Sigma_{j\in S''}v_j-\Sigma_{j\in S}v_j=v_{r_n}-v_{\hat{s}}>0$. ■

The second property confirms that the matroid property captures the notion of substitutes. Informally, goods are substitutes in demand if increasing the cost of item n does not cause another item $m\neq n$ to be rejected. In the present model, we impose that condition on the portion of the value/cost domain for which the optimum is unique: if $m\in A^*(v_1,\ldots,v_n,\ldots,v_N)$ and $m\neq n$, then for all $v_n'>v_n$, $m\in A^*(v_1,\ldots,v_n',\ldots,v_N)$.

Proposition 2.15

If $\mathcal{R}$ is a matroid, then the goods in problem (7) are substitutes. Conversely, if $\mathcal{R}$ has properties 1 and 2 but not the augmentation property, then the goods in problem (7) are *not* substitutes.

Proof

Assume that $\mathcal{R}$ is a matroid. Take v' such that $v'_n > v_n$ and $v'_i = v_i$ for $i \neq n$. Assume that there is some $m \notin R^*(v)$ with $m \neq n$, such that $m \in R^*(v')$. We show that this leads to a contradiction.

First, let $\hat{m}$ be the least valuable of such m, that is, $v_m \geq v_{\hat{m}}$ for all $m \in R^*(v') - R^*(v)$. As argued earlier, $|R^*(v)| = |R^*(v')|$ and so $\left|R^*(v)\right| > \left|R^*(v') - \{\hat{m}\}\right|$. By augmentation, there exists $k \in R^*(v) - \left(R^*(v') - \{\hat{m}\}\right)$ such that $\left(R^*(v') - \{\hat{m}\}\right) \cup \{k\} \in \mathcal{R}$ and optimality of $R^*(v')$ implies $v'_{\hat{m}} > v'_k$. Thus, $v_m > v'_k$ for all $m \in R^*(v') - R^*(v)$. On the other hand, $|R^*(v')| > |R^*(v) - \{k\}|$ and for some $\tilde{m} \in R^*(v') - \left(R^*(v) - \{k\}\right)$, we have $\left(R^*(v) - \{k\}\right) \cup \{\tilde{m}\} \in \mathcal{R}$. This time, optimality of $R^*(v)$ implies $v_k > v_{\tilde{m}}$. But then, $v_k > v_{\tilde{m}} \geq v_m > v'_k$, a contradiction.

Conversely, if properties 1 and 2 hold but 3 does not, then there exist $S, S' \in \mathcal{R}$ with $|S| > |S'|$ such that for all $x \in S - S'$ we have $S' \cup \{x\} \notin \mathcal{R}$. For each $x \in S$, let $v_x = 1$ and for all $x \notin S$, let $v_x = 0$. With these values v, there is an optimum of (7) with $R^*(v) = S$. One by one, increase the values of the items $x \in S'$ each to $|S|+1$, so $S' \subseteq R^*(v')$. By the failure of augmentation, $S' = R^*(v')$. Hence, at least one value increase resulted in two or more items being added to A^*. That is, for some n such that $v'_n > v_n$, two different elements satisfy $m', m \in A^*(v_1, \ldots v_n, \ldots, v_N)$ and $m, m' \notin A^*(v_1, \ldots v'_n, \ldots, v_N)$. We know either $m \neq n$ or $m' \neq n$, violating the substitutes condition. ■

We can compare the model of this section to the Kelso-Crawford model studied earlier. In the Kelso-Crawford model, "firms" were the buyers and "workers" were the goods to be purchased (hired). In this section, there is just one buyer, corresponding to the special case of the Kelso-Crawford model with just one firm. To make the formulations closer, let us suppose that the model of this section is revised to add an explicit value of goods/workers to the buyer. Let that value be the same for any acceptable set of goods/workers, and make it at least $\Sigma_{i=1}^{N} v_i$. For unacceptable sets, the value is zero. This specification ensures that it is optimal for the one firm to buy/hire an acceptable set, provided that one is available. Proposition 2.15 affirms that goods are substitutes for firms, as required by the Kelso-Crawford model. So, the conclusion of the Kelso-Crawford model about ascending auctions—that it achieves an efficient allocation—applies. In this case, that means that the outcome maximizes the total value.

Intuitively, the greedy rejection algorithm studied in this section is "dual" to the Kelso-Crawford auction algorithm. It works by rejecting the most expensive items until no more can be rejected, while the Kelso-Crawford algorithm works by hiring ("accepting") the most desirable workers until no more workers are wanted. In all the models presented in this chapter, a substitutes condition makes it possible for the prices and values to work in either direction, starting from low prices/values and raising them until enough offers are accepted or starting with high prices/values and reducing them until enough offers are rejected.

Our key findings in this section are the following:

- A particular greedy algorithm can be defined to apply to a superset of the set of knapsack problems, to encompass arbitrary sets of constraints.
    - This algorithm successively rejects the most expensive remaining item, so long as doing so is feasible.
    - The algorithm is monotonic, and the corresponding threshold auction is strategy-proof.
- When the collection of sets of goods that can be feasibly rejected are given,
    - The substitutes condition for goods is characterized by the matroid condition for sets of rejected goods, and
    - the greedy rejection algorithm applied to the substitutes case produces an optimal allocation.
- Because the matroid condition characterizes substitutes, this model can be considered a special case of the Kelso-Crawford model. Its special characteristics are that:
    - There is a single firm (plus a more detailed modeling of the firm's demand).
    - The firm's constraints determine the sets of items that can be accepted or rejected.
    - The value of acquiring a sufficient set of individual items is very high, but there is no value to exceeding sufficiency.
    - Consequently, the firm seeks to minimize the "cost" or "value" of the items it acquires or, equivalently, to maximize the cost or value of the items it rejects.

3

VICKREY AUCTIONS AND SUBSTITUTION

Although auctions have been used by people for millennia, the theoretical analysis of auctions in economics is much more recent, dating back to the work by William Vickrey (1961), who also introduced a new kind of auction for some hard resource-allocation problems. Vickrey wanted to know whether one could eliminate the gaming in auctions to make the outcomes more certain and to make bidding easier for participants. His theoretical ideas were extended by Groves (1973) and Clarke (1971) to apply to public goods problems, and a back-formation led to the generalization of Vickrey's work that is now mostly known as the "Vickrey auction."

A Vickrey auction is a "direct mechanism," which means that bidders are asked to report what they know, which is called their "types." For example, in an auction to buy a single good, a bidder's type might be the highest price it would be willing to pay for the item, and it would be asked to report that. What is surprising about the Vickrey auction is that truthful reporting is always optimal for each bidder, no matter what the other bidders may report. An auction with that property is said to be strategy-proof.

The magic that makes a Vickrey auction strategy-proof is the way the payments are determined from the bids. The most famous of the Vickrey auctions is one that applies when there is a single good for sale. Each potential buyer is asked to report, or "bid," the highest price that it would be willing to pay. Unlike the most common auction that readers may know—the so-called "sealed tender"—the winning bidder in a Vickrey auction does not pay a price equal to amount that it had bid. The item is awarded to the highest bidder, but the price is set equal to the second-highest bid. Any reader who has not seen this before is encouraged to work through the logic, both to see that it is indeed optimal from each bidder's perspective to report truthfully and to see why that fact may not be immediately obvious to real bidders, who sometimes make mistakes in such an auction.

How can that finding be generalized to a case in which there may be multiple, heterogeneous goods for sale? We will treat this formally later, but intuitively, the general Vickrey auction works as follows: Each bidder is asked to submit information, or "bids," to describe its value for every relevant outcome. The auctioneer then treats that reported information as truthful and uses it to compute the outcome with the highest possible value. Finally, the auctioneer determines the payments. The Vickrey payments are what most distinguish the Vickrey auction. Suppose that if bidder n does not participate in the auction, the total value of the goods that other bidders get would be π_{-n}. If bidder n participates and wins something, the total value it gets is some smaller amount π'_{-n}.

In a Vickrey auction, bidder n pays $\pi_{-n} - \pi'_{-n}$, which is just sufficient so that the total value received by others, including the auctioneer, is still π_{-n}, that is, it is unaffected by n's participation.

By setting n's payment in that way, whatever effect bidder n may have on the auctioneer's choice of outcome cannot influence the total payoff to everyone else. Consequently, for bidder n to maximize its own payoff, it must convince the auctioneer to maximize the total payoff to all participants (including bidder n's actual payoff). Given the way the auctioneer chooses the outcome, the bidder can accomplish that by reporting its own value truthfully.

Two restrictions on analysis are apparent in the formulation in the next section. First, n's cost depends only on what n knows, and never on what anybody else knows. This is called the "private values" assumption and is crucial to the analysis. Second, n's cost depends only on what n acquires and not on what others may acquire. This restriction is not needed for the formal analysis but makes it easier to tell the story of how the auction works.

3.1 MODEL, DEFINITION, AND STRATEGY-PROOFNESS FOR THE VICKREY AUCTION

I represent a general, abstract auction problem with one auctioneer, who can be a buyer or a seller. For concreteness, let us say that the auctioneer is a buyer and that there are N bidders (sellers), labeled by $n = 1, \ldots, N$. Each seller can offer to sell goods or services $x_n \in X_n$. For example, if seller n can offer a red widget or a green widget (but not both) or nothing, then we model that by setting $X_n = \{R, G, \varnothing\}$. If the seller can offer zero, one, or two green widgets and zero or one red widgets or any combination, then there are six feasible combinations in total, and we could set $X_n = \{\varnothing, (0,1), (1,0), (1,1), (2,0), (2,1)\}$. Here $\varnothing$ represents $(0,0)$. The X_n notation is very flexible, but we do require that the set X_n be finite[1] and contain $\varnothing$, a "null" element that represents providing nothing and incurring a cost of zero.

Each seller n will have some cost associated with supplying goods or services. I assume that the seller knows that cost but that others may not know it. To model uncertainty about each seller n, I introduce a random variable θ_n, which takes values in some set Θ_n and which parameterizes the seller's cost function. This random variable θ_n is called the seller's "type," and each other participant in the auction has beliefs about that, characterized by some probability distribution. Thus, any seller n's cost is described by the parameterized function $C : X_n \times \Theta_n \rightarrow \mathbb{R}_+$. I normalize C so that $C(\varnothing, \theta_n) = 0$ for all θ_n. A seller's payoff π_n from participating in the mechanism and providing goods x_n is the total price p_n that it receives, minus its total cost: $\pi_n = p_n - C(x_n, \theta_n)$.

Next, consider the buyer. The set of possible combinations of things that the buyer might feasibly acquire is $X_0 = X_1 \times \cdots \times X_N$, with typical combination $x_0 \stackrel{\text{def}}{=} (x_1, \ldots, x_N)$. The buyer's value for each combination is described by $v : X_0 \rightarrow \mathbb{R}$, and its payoff when it buys x_0 is the value of what it acquires minus what it must pay: $\pi_0 = v(x_0) - \Sigma_{n=1}^{N} p_n$.

For x_0, the total surplus is enjoyed by all the parties, including the buyer: $TS(x_0, \theta) = v(x_0) - \Sigma_{n=1}^{N} C(x_n, \theta_n)$. Notice that the payments cancel in this expression: the payment p_n increases bidder n's payoff but reduces the buyer's payoff by an equal amount. Let $TS^*(\theta) = \max_{x_0 \in X_0} TS(x_0, \theta)$.

For the Vickrey payment formula, observe that if we omit one participant m, the maximum total payoff to others is $TS^*_{-m}(\theta_{-m}) \stackrel{\text{def}}{=} \max_{x_0 \in X_0, x_m = \varnothing} \left(v(x_0) - \Sigma_{n \neq m} C(x_n, \theta_n)\right)$. So for the Vickrey mechanism to ensure that the total payoff enjoyed by other participants is $TS^*_{-m}(\theta_{-m})$, regardless of m's report, m's payoff must be $TS^*(\theta) - TS^*_{-m}(\theta_{-m})$, so its payment must be that amount plus its cost.

Definition

The Vickrey mechanism is the direct mechanism in which:

1. Each bidder n reports information θ_n to the auctioneer.
2. The auctioneer uses the reported information to select an outcome $x_0^*(\theta) \in \max_{x_0 \in X_0} v(x_0) - \Sigma_{n=1}^{N} C(x_n, \theta_n)$.
3. The auctioneer pays bidder m the amount

$$p_m^*(\theta) \stackrel{\text{def}}{=} TS^*(\theta) - TS^*_{-m}(\theta_{-m}) + C\left(x_m^*(\theta), \theta_m\right). \qquad (8)$$

If m fails to report truthfully, this may cause the decision to change in a way that reduces the total surplus. Since the total accruing to the others is not affected, that can only harm m. The consequence is that the sellers all have an incentive to report truthfully.

Proposition 3.1

The Vickrey auction is strategy-proof: that is, for all θ and all m, $\theta_m \in argmax_{\hat{\theta}_m}\ p_m^*(\hat{\theta}_m, \theta_{-m}) - C\left(x_m^*(\hat{\theta}_m, \theta_{-m}), \theta_m\right)$.

Proof

For any $\hat{\theta}_m$, let us compute the change in m's payoff by reporting $\hat{\theta}_m$ instead of the truthful report θ_m:

$$\left(p_m^*(\hat{\theta}_m, \theta_{-m}) - C\left(x_m^*(\hat{\theta}_m, \theta_{-m}), \theta_m\right)\right)$$
$$-\left(p_m^*(\theta_m, \theta_{-m}) - C\left(x_m^*(\theta_m, \theta_{-m}), \theta_m\right)\right)$$

$$= \left(v\left(x_0^*(\hat{\theta}_m, \theta_{-m})\right) - \Sigma_{n=1}^N C\left(x_n^*(\hat{\theta}_m, \theta_{-m}), \theta_n\right) - \pi_{-m}(\theta_{-m})\right)$$
$$-\left(v\left(x_0^*(\theta)\right) - \Sigma_{n=1}^N C\left(x_n^*(\theta), \theta_n\right) - \pi_{-m}(\theta_{-m})\right) \leq 0.$$

The first step proceeds by substituting the Vickrey payment formula into the initial line and reorganizing terms. Second, the inequality is implied, because, by definition, $x_0^*(\theta) \in argmax_{x_0 \in X_0}\ v(x_0) - \Sigma_{n=1}^N C(x_n, \theta_n)$. So player m can only lose by misreporting: $p_m^*(\hat{\theta}_m, \theta_{-m}) - C\left(x_m^*(\hat{\theta}_m, \theta_{-m}), \theta_m\right) \leq p_m^*(\theta_m, \theta_{-m}) - C\left(x_m^*(\theta_m, \theta_{-m}), \theta_m\right)$.■

3.2 UNIQUENESS OF PAYMENT RULES FOR STRATEGY-PROOF MECHANISMS

Why do we place so much emphasis on clever Vickrey payment rules? A famous result of Green and Laffont (1977), generalized by Holmström (1979), establishes that, for certain classes of environments, the Vickrey payments are the *only* ones consistent with a strategy-proof auction that implements the value-maximizing decision $x_0^*(\theta)$. Although we found earlier that the greedy and truncated greedy threshold auctions are strategy-proof (as are all threshold auctions in those environments), those mechanisms are not exceptions, because they do not generally entail the value-maximizing decision.

In this section, we verify that, for any allocation rule α, there is at most one payment rule p^α such that the direct mechanism (α, p^α) is strategy-proof. This proposition implies the Green-Laffont-Holmström conclusion, formalizes the claim about the uniqueness of threshold auctions, and provides some guidance about the possibility of constructing strategy-proof mechanisms for other environments.

Before limiting our attention to "auctions," we discuss the result for a wider class of strategy-proof direct mechanisms.

Formally, a *direct mechanism* is a pair (α, p^α). The formalism is meant to describe a situation in which each bidder n makes a report $\hat{\theta}_n$, which is understood to mean that the bidder claims that its type is $\hat{\theta}_n$. The auctioneer then uses the reported information to select an outcome $\alpha(\hat{\theta}) \in X_0$ and determines payments $p_n^\alpha(\hat{\theta})$ to each bidder n. If bidder n reports falsely, that means that $\hat{\theta}_n \neq \theta_n$. In the formal treatment that follows, the notation *argmax* refers to the set of arguments that maximize a specified objective. If the mechanism is strategy-proof, then in the description given, we see a term like $\theta_n \in argmax\ldots$, which means that the truthful reporting maximizes the bidder's payoff, so nothing can be gained by reporting falsely.

Definition

1. A direct mechanism is a pair of functions $(\alpha, p^{\alpha}): \Theta_1 \times \ldots \times \Theta_N \to X_0 \times \mathbb{R}^N$.
2. The direct mechanism (α, p^{α}) is *strategy-proof* if, for all n and $\theta \in \Theta_1 \times \ldots \times \Theta_N$,

$$\theta_n \in argmax_{\hat{\theta}_n \in \Theta_n}\ p_n^{\alpha}(\hat{\theta}_n, \theta_{-n}) - C\left(\alpha(\hat{\theta}_n, \theta_{-n}), \theta_n\right).$$

The analysis in this section relies on an assumption about the class of environments that is innocent for all of our intended applications. The assumption is that C must be a continuously differentiable function of its parameter $\theta_n \in \Theta_n$, and the set Θ_n must be path connected. To keep the treatment elementary, we further limit attention to the case in which, for all n, $\Theta_n = [0, 1]$.

Proposition 3.2

Let $\Theta_n = [0, 1]$ for $n = 1, \ldots, N$, and suppose that $C(x, \theta_n)$ is continuously differentiable in its second argument with partial derivative $C_2(x, \theta_n) = \frac{\partial C}{\partial \theta_n}(x, \theta_n)$. Let (α, p^{α}) be a strategy-proof direct mechanism. Then there exist functions $\beta_n : \Theta_{-n} \to \mathbb{R}$ such that, for all n and θ,

$$p_n^{\alpha}(\theta) = C\left(\alpha(\theta), \theta_n\right) + \int_0^{\theta_n} C_2\left(\alpha(s, \theta_{-n}), s\right) ds + \beta_n(\theta_{-n}). \quad (9)$$

Proof

Let $V_n(\theta) \stackrel{\text{def}}{=} \max_{\hat{\theta}_n \in \Theta_n} p_n^{\alpha}(\hat{\theta}_n, \theta_{-n}) - C\left(\alpha(\hat{\theta}_n, \theta_{-n}), \theta_n\right)$. Since the mechanism is strategy-proof, $V_n(\theta) = p_\theta^{\alpha}(\theta) - C\left(\alpha(\theta), \theta_n\right)$. According to the "integral form" envelope theorem of Milgrom and Segal (2002), a second expression for the value is $V_n(\theta) = V_n\left(0, \theta_{-n}\right) + \int_0^{\theta_n} C_2\left(\alpha(s, \theta_{-n}), s\right) ds$. Equating these two expressions and setting $\beta_n(\theta_{-n}) = V_n(0, \theta_{-n})$ proves the result. ■

In auction applications, we often limit attention to environments in which each bidder can refuse to participate and, by doing so, get a payoff of zero. We model that by adding the restriction that there is some type, say type 0, such that reporting that type results in the seller getting a payoff of zero (presumably because it receives zero payments and incurs zero costs). Studying the preceding proof, we find that this amounts to adding the restriction that $\beta(\theta_{-n}) = 0$, in which case there can be at most one price function p^{α} such that (α, p^{α}) is a strategy-proof direct-auction mechanism.

Proposition 3.3

Let $\Theta_n = [0, 1]$ for $n = 1, \ldots, N$, and suppose that $C(x, \theta_n)$ is continuously differentiable in its second argument with partial derivative $C_2(x, \theta_n) = \frac{\partial C}{\partial \theta_n}(x, \theta_n)$. Let (α, p^{α}) be a strategy-proof direct mechanism, and suppose that for all n and θ_{-n}, $p_n^{\alpha}(0, \theta_{-n}) - C\left(\alpha(0, \theta_{-n}), 0\right) = 0$. Then, $p_n^{\alpha}(\theta) = C\left(\alpha(\theta), \theta_n\right) + \int_0^{\theta_n} C_2\left(\alpha(s, \theta_{-n}), s\right) ds$.[2]

Although we have stated and proved the two propositions only for the type spaces $\Theta_n = [0, 1]$, these propositions imply similar payment restrictions along any one-dimensional path in any subspace of a path-connected Θ_n, from which we may infer that the conclusion holds for any path-connected sets Θ_n.

In particular, proposition 3.3 proves that there is only one payment, namely $p_n^\alpha(\theta)$, that results in implementing any particular winner selection rule in a strategy-proof way. So, the Vickrey payments are the only ones to implement the efficient outcome in a strategy-proof way, subject to the assumptions about the auction environment.

3.3 THE CORE AS A COMPETITIVE STANDARD

What should be our standard for a "good" outcome in a decentralized complex allocation problem? On one hand, efficiency is important: we would like a chosen allocation to achieve the maximum value if possible, or something near to the maximum. A separate question is how the value should be shared. As we have seen earlier, sharing value in an appropriate way encourages value-creating investments, and competitive pricing is an economist's natural first guess about how to do that.

In this section, I argue that the *core*, which is a standard concept of coalitional game theory, is a suitable notion of *competitive* payoffs for auction problems. It is the one that not only says that outcomes are efficient but also that competition among the participants limits how much each can demand from the others.

Intuitively, a core outcome is characterized by competition for the services of the several participants, who have skills or resources that create value in the items being sold. If the sellers and buyer in the auction were available for hire by a set of external parties (or by one another) in a competitive market, then the market-clearing competitive prices—the fixed payments that parties would have to offer in addition to costs to hire the participants—are exactly the payoff vectors in the core of the coalitional game. To make this formal, we need to specify certain details.

Imagine that we introduce a new set of players, whom we call "outsiders," seeking to hire the services of the participants in the auction: the buyer (player 0) and the sellers. Suppose that anyone who succeeds in hiring the buyer and a collection of sellers $S \subseteq \mathcal{N} \stackrel{\text{def}}{=} \{1, \ldots, N\}$ can ask its sellers to choose a productive action $x_S = (x_n)_{n \in S}$, provided it compensates them for their individual costs $C(x_n, \theta_n)$. Here we extend the definition of v to accept as an argument any such x_S and say that $v(x_S) \stackrel{\text{def}}{=} v(x_S, \varnothing_{-S})$, that is, bidders $i \notin S$ are treated as supplying $\varnothing$.

The maximum value that the outsiders can create from acquiring the buyer and some set of sellers S is summarized by the *coalition-value function*:[3]

$$c(S) = \max_{x_S} v(x_S) - \Sigma_{n \in S} C(x_n, \theta_n). \qquad (10)$$

The outsiders act as price takers, and since each seller n can produce $x_n = \varnothing$ at zero cost, the greatest total value is achieved by the whole set of sellers:

$$c(\mathcal{N}) = \max_{x_{\mathcal{N}}} v(x_{\mathcal{N}}) - \Sigma_{n \in \mathcal{N}} C(x_n, \theta_n) = \max_{S \subseteq \mathcal{N}} c(S).$$

What would the market prices of the auction buyer and sellers have to be for market clearing in a competitive market of this sort? Suppose the outsiders promise to pay π_n to each participant hired (in addition to whatever cost the participant may incur by following the outsider's instructions). Competition must drive the outsiders' profits to zero, so in equilibrium there cannot be a strictly positive profit from hiring the buyer and any set of suppliers S:

$$c(S)-\pi_0-\sum_{n\in S}\pi_n\leq 0,$$

and since it is efficient for one outsider to hire everyone, doing that in equilibrium must lead to profits of exactly zero:

$$c(\mathcal{N})-\pi_0-\sum_{n\in\mathcal{N}}\pi_n=0.$$

By definition, in a coalitional game with players $\mathcal{N}\cup\{0\}$ and in which zero is the value of a coalition without the buyer and $c(S)$ is the value a coalition with the buyer and sellers in S, the core $core(\mathcal{N}\cup\{0\},c)$ is exactly the set of payoffs satisfying the preceding two conditions.

$$core(\mathcal{N}\cup\{0\},c)\overset{\text{def}}{=}\Big\{\pi\in\mathbb{R}_+^{N+1}\,|\,\pi_0+\Sigma_{n\in\mathcal{N}}\pi_n=c(\mathcal{N}),$$
$$(\forall S\subseteq\mathcal{N})\,\pi_0+\Sigma_{n\in S}\pi_n\geq c(S)\Big\}. \quad (11)$$

This provides a formal justification for the claim that the core represents a set of competitive payoffs.

For the analysis to follow, it is sometimes helpful to describe an equivalent formula, in which the constraints are stated as upper bounds on the total payoff to any set of bidders. One can move back and forth between the upper- and lower-bound constraints by applying the equation that is the first part of the definition of the core.

$$core(\mathcal{N} \cup \{0\}, c) = \Big\{ \pi \in \mathbb{R}_{+}^{N+1} \mid \pi_0 + \sum\nolimits_{n \in \mathcal{N}} \pi_n$$

$$= c(\mathcal{N}), (\forall S \subseteq \mathcal{N}) \sum\nolimits_{n \in S} \pi_n \leq c(\mathcal{N}) - c(\mathcal{N} - S) \Big\}. \quad (12)$$

3.4 WHEN VICKREY PAYOFFS ARE NOT IN THE CORE

Vickrey auctions do not always lead to payoffs in the core.

Example

The buyer needs to acquire two items and is willing, if necessary, to pay up to twenty-five for them. The buyer has no value for just one item.

There are three sellers, each of which can set up a machine at a cost of ten to manufacture the two items. However, seller 1 and seller 2 each has an item in inventory, where it is otherwise worthless, so the cost of supplying one item is zero for those two sellers and ten for seller 3.

Given these costs, the Vickrey outcome x_0 chooses sellers 1 and 2 each to supply one item, because the associated cost is zero. The Vickrey price paid to each seller, however, is ten, so the buyer's total cost is twenty, and the buyer's payoff is five.

The Vickrey outcome is troubling, for if the buyer had decided to buy from just one supplier and taken bids for a pair of items, each would have reported a cost of ten, and the total price would be ten, and its payoff would be fifteen. The same outcome would be the equilibrium outcome of a descending auction for a pair of items, in which currently losing sellers get an opportunity to reduce their prices to be more competitive, until no seller is willing to go any lower. The buyer's Vickrey payoff seems too low to be competitive, and the sellers' payoffs seem too high.

We can also analyze the competitive pricing question using the concept of the core. The buyer and sellers 1 and 2 can get to the efficient allocation by themselves, so (omitting commas): $c(12) = c(123) = 25$. So, by the definition of the core, we have $\pi_0 + \pi_1 + \pi_2 + \pi_3 = 25$, and $\pi_0 + \pi_1 + \pi_2 \geq 25$, and $\pi_3 \geq 0$. So the inequalities are tight, implying that $\pi_3 = 0$. Also, $\pi_0 + \pi_3 \geq c(3) = 15$, so $\pi_0 \geq 15$. Translated into words, this means in the core, the buyer's payoff must be at least fifteen, and the cost of the two items for the buyer must not exceed ten.

In general, when Vickrey outcomes are not in the core, the reason is that the payoff to the auctioneer (in these examples, the buyer) is too low. The following general statement of that result was reported by Ausubel and Milgrom (2002).

Proposition 3.4

Each bidder's Vickrey payoff is equal to its highest payoff over all points in the core: $\pi_n^* = \max_{\gamma \in Core(\mathcal{N} \cup \{0\}, c)} \gamma_n$ for $n = 1, \ldots, N$. In particular, for any $\gamma \in core(\mathcal{N} \cup \{0\}, c)$, $\pi_0^* \leq \gamma_0$.

Proof

Notice that the c notation provides a convenient shorthand for describing a bidder's Vickrey profit: $\pi_n^* = c(\mathcal{N}) - c(\mathcal{N} - \{n\})$. Also, using equation (12) for the singleton set $\{n\}$, for any point γ in the core, $\gamma_n \le c(\mathcal{N}) - c(\mathcal{N} - \{n\}) = \pi_n^*$. Moreover, the payoff vector γ', with $\gamma'_n = \pi_n^*, \gamma'_0 = c(\mathcal{N}) - \pi_n^*$, and otherwise $\gamma'_m = 0$, is, by inspection, in the core. ■

3.5 VICKREY AUCTIONS AND INVESTMENT INCENTIVES

An advantage of the Vickrey auction is that it can provide excellent incentives for *individual* bidders to make investments, given the investments of others. However, in general, Vickrey auctions still allow coordination problems among bidders to lead to inefficient investments.

For the positive result about *individual* incentives, suppose that bidder 1 can, by investing an amount i_1, change its type from θ_1 to θ'_1, which would change the Vickrey decision from $x_0^*(\theta)$ to $x_0^*(\theta')$, where $\theta' \stackrel{\text{def}}{=} (\theta'_1, \theta_{-1})$. To maximize its own payoff, bidder 1 will choose to make that investment if $p_1^*(\theta) - C\left(x_1^*(\theta), \theta_1\right) < p_1^*(\theta') - C\left(x_1^*(\theta'), \theta'_1\right) - i_1$. Substituting the Vickrey payment formula and using algebra to simplify, we can restate the condition as $v\left(x_0^*(\theta)\right) - \Sigma_{n\in\mathcal{N}} C(x_n, \theta_n) < v\left(x_0^*(\theta')\right) - \Sigma_{n\in\mathcal{N}} C(x_n, \theta'_n) - i_1$. That, however, is precisely the condition under which making the investment increases total payoffs for all participants and the auctioneer. Of course, the same is true for any bidder m. That proves the following proposition.

Proposition 3.5

In a Vickrey auction, an individual bidder *m* can gain by investing, given the other bidders' types, exactly when that investment increases the total value for all participants. Formally:

$$\left[p_m^*(\theta) - C\left(x_m^*(\theta), \theta_m\right) < p_m^*(\theta') - C\left(x_m^*(\theta'), \theta_m'\right) - i_m\right]$$

$$\Leftrightarrow \left[v\left(x_0^*(\theta)\right) - \sum_{n \in \mathcal{N}} C(x_n, \theta_n) < v\left(x_0^*(\theta')\right) - \sum_{n \in \mathcal{N}} C(x_n, \theta_n') - i_m\right]$$

The intuition for proposition 3.5 again highlights the nature of Vickrey payments. These are computed so that if *m* changes its reported type from θ_m to θ_m', that has zero effect on the total payoff to the other participants. Consequently, the difference in *m*'s payoffs in the first line is equal to the difference in total payoffs in the second line.

To focus on bidder investments, we formulate a simplified game, in which each bidder *n* is endowed with some investment option and chooses whether to exercise it. Each bidder has a binary choice: invest or don't invest. The model omits the bidder's reporting choice in the Vickrey auction and instead computes the payoffs as if each player were certain to play its dominant strategy in the Vickrey auction. A strategy profile in this game is an element $\sigma \in \{\text{invest, don't invest}\}^N$. Let σ^* denote the profile of investment decisions that maximizes the total payoff. Then, proposition 3.5 immediately implies the following:

Proposition 3.6

The efficient investment profile σ^* is a pure Nash equilibrium of the investment game.

Despite this positive result, there is a problem: there can also be inefficient Nash equilibria of the investment game.

Example 1

Suppose a buyer seeks to acquire two units of a good and has a value of ten for the pair and zero for anything less. Sellers 1 and 2 individually can each produce nothing. However, each can, by investing 1, gain the ability to produce one unit at cost two. Then, maximum total value of four is achieved if both sellers invest and bid truthfully, and in that case the Vickrey prices are eight and eight. However, neither seller finds it profitable to invest unless the other seller invests as well.

In normal form, the game looks as shown in the table. The rows correspond to decisions by seller 1 and the columns to decisions by seller 2. The first number in each cell is seller 1's payoff; the second, seller 2's payoff; and the third is the buyer's payoff.

	Invest	Don't invest
Invest	5, 5, −6	−1, 0, 0
Don't invest	0, −1, 0	0, 0, 0

There are *two* pure Nash equilibria along the main diagonal of the payoff matrix: (invest, invest) and (don't invest, don't invest). This pattern is a typical "coordination failure," and in this example it leads to underinvestment. Notice that the Vickrey prices following (invest, invest) are so high (eight for each seller) that the buyer loses six on the deal: it pays a total price of sixteen and gets items that it believes are worth just ten. This is an example of a payoff vector outside the core.

Besides the two pure equilibria, the game also has a mixed equilibrium in which each seller invests with probability $\frac{1}{6}$ and has a zero expected payoff in this equilibrium.

In example 1, the two sellers provide complementary inputs that are only valuable when used together, and the result is that equilibrium can involve little investment. Other kinds of inefficiencies are possible as well and can arise even when goods are substitutes. Here is such an example.

Example 2

Suppose a buyer seeks to acquire one unit of a good and has a value of ten for it. Sellers 1 and 2 individually can produce nothing without making an investment, or either can make an investment to gain the ability to produce one unit at cost two. The cost to make an investment is one for seller 1 and two for seller 2, so the efficient outcome has seller 1 invest and seller 2 not invest. As in the previous example, seller 1 is the row player; seller 2 is the column player; and the third number is the buyer's payoff.

	Invest	**Don't invest**
Invest	−1, −2, 8	7, 0, 0
Don't invest	0, 6, 0	0, 0, 0

Again, there are two pure Nash equilibria, but this time they occupy the opposite diagonal. Thus, in both equilibria, one party invests and the other does not. The equilibrium in which seller 2, which has higher investment costs, makes the investment is wasteful: it fails to maximize total payoffs. Besides the two pure equilibria, there is also a mixed equilibrium in which seller 1 invests with probability ¾ and seller 2 invests with probability ⅞, and in equilibrium both sellers earn zero expected payoffs.

Thus, our general findings about investment incentives are mixed. Individual incentives point in the right direction, in the limited sense that each seller, given the investments of the others, chooses its own investment in a way consistent with maximizing the total payoff. But the examples highlight two ways in which inefficiency can happen anyway. In the first, the investments are complementary, and each investor is unsure about the other. If one player expects the other to refrain from investing, then it will refrain, too, leading to an inefficient outcome. In the second example, there is room for just one investor, and if either invests, then competition makes it unprofitable for the second one to invest as well. In the second example, the wrong party can invest, and there is no force at work to avoid or correct that inefficiency.

3.6 VICKREY PAYOFFS WHEN GOODS ARE SUBSTITUTES

In our example with payoffs outside the core, seller 1's inventory is of no value to the system unless seller 2's inventory is also present: their goods are complements. That was no accident: substitutes turn out to be just the right condition to characterize when Vickrey payoffs can be "guaranteed" to lie in the core. The precise statements are tricky, involving careful quantifications, so the sophisticated reader should attend to those details in the propositions stated later.

The following results are stated using a formulation in which sellers might offer distinct or identical goods and the buyer seeks to acquire some collection of goods. There are L distinct kinds of goods, so the collection is represented by a vector $\overline{x} \in \mathbb{R}_+^L$, and seller n supplies a vector $x_n \in \mathbb{R}_+^L$. The buyer has a vector of values for the goods denoted by $P \in \mathbb{R}_+^L$. This may represent the buyer's costs of producing each good for itself or procuring them outside the auction, or its opportunity cost of substituting other goods, or the loss from scaling back operations if the good cannot be acquired.

In contrast to the models formulated earlier, in this model the sellers may provide multiple kinds of goods, and some kinds may be provided by more than one seller.

3.6.1 VICKREY FORMULATION WITH GOODS

We consider an environment in which when the buyer acquires goods $\Sigma_{n=1}^N x_n \le \overline{x} \in \mathbb{R}_+^L$ from sellers $n = 1, \ldots, N$; its value is $v(x) = P \cdot \Sigma_{n=1}^N x_n$. It has no additional value for goods in excess of $\overline{x}$. The Vickrey allocation is this:

$$x_0^*(\theta) \in argmax_{x \in \mathbb{R}_+^{NL}} \sum_{i=1}^{L} P_i \min\left(\overline{x}_i, \sum_{n=1}^{N} x_{ni}\right)$$
$$- \sum_{n=1}^{N} C(x_n, \theta_n).$$

We find that when goods are substitutes for the bidders, the Vickrey outcome is in the core, so the seller's revenue is not uncompetitively low for such cases. To develop this result formally and see the extent to which some condition like substitutes is necessary, we need two more definitions. The first definition is motivated by the idea that the Vickrey payoff may depend on which bidders actually participate in the auction. As we have seen previously, just by substituting the Vickrey payments into the payoff formula, we can write bidder n's Vickrey payoff as $\pi_n^* = c(\mathcal{N}) - c(\mathcal{N} - \{n\})$. We will write the same formula for other sets of bidders. Also, we want to define a condition that identifies this difference as decreasing when we augment the set of bidders.

Definitions

1. If the set of bidders participating in an auction is denoted by S, then the Vickrey payoff for bidder $n \in S$ is $\pi_n^*(S) \stackrel{\text{def}}{=} c(S) - c(S - \{n\})$.
2. The coalition values are said to be *bidder submodular* if, for any set of bidders S and any pair of bidders $n, n' \in S$, $c(S) - c(S - \{n\}) \leq c(S - \{n'\}) - c(S - \{n, n'\})$ (or, equivalently, $n \in S \subset T$ implies $\pi_n^*(T) \leq \pi_n^*(S)$).

There are two main results associated with these definitions. Both are due to Ausubel and Milgrom (2002).

Proposition 3.7

In the Vickrey formulation with goods, for every $S \subseteq \mathcal{N}$, $\pi^*(S) \in core(S \cup \{0\}, c)$ if, and only if, the coalition values are bidder submodular.

Thus, the bidder submodularity condition is sufficient and, in a particular sense, also necessary. Given a set of bidders, if we are not sure which ones will participate in the auction, then we can be sure that the Vickrey outcome will be in the core only if the coalition values are bidder submodular.

Proposition 3.8

In the Vickrey formulation with goods, if goods are substitutes in each seller's cost function, then coalition values are bidder submodular.

Proposition 3.8 has a converse as well, as developed in Milgrom (2004), but we omit that from this treatment.

We prove proposition 3.7 by elementary methods. The simplest proof of proposition 3.8 uses duality theory and can be skipped for an elementary treatment.

Proof of Proposition 3.7

Suppose the coalition values are bidder submodular and fix S. We need to prove that any $S' \subseteq S$ satisfies the second condition of equation (12). If $|S'| = 1$, say, $S' = \{m'\}$, then by definition 1, $\pi^*_{m'}(S) \leq c(S) - c(S - \{m'\})$. Suppose that for any $|S'| = n \geq 1$, $\Sigma_{m' \in S'} \pi^*_{m'} \leq c(S) - c(S - S')$ holds. Then, for any S' such that $|S'| = n + 1$:

$$\begin{aligned}\sum_{m' \in S'} \pi^*_{m'}(S) = \pi^*_m(S) + \sum_{m' \in \{S' - \{m\}\}} \pi^*_{m'}(S)\\ \leq c(S) - c(S - (S' - \{m\})) + \pi^*_m(S)\\ \leq c(S) - c(S - (S' - \{m\})) + \pi^*_m(S - (S' - \{m\}))\\ = c(S) - c(S \setminus S')\end{aligned}$$

where the second inequality comes from submodularity. We can conclude that $\forall S' \subset S, \Sigma_{m' \in S'} \pi^*_{m'}(S) \leq c(S) - c(S - S')$. Thus, for all $S \subseteq \mathcal{N}, \pi^*(S) \in core\left(S \cup \{0\}, c\right)$.

Conversely, suppose the coalition values are not bidder submodular. Then there exists a coalition S and bidders $n, n' \in S$, where $c(S) - c\left(S - \{n\}\right) > c\left(S - \{n'\}\right) - c\left(S - \{n, n'\}\right)$. But then:

$$\begin{aligned}\pi^*_n(S) + \pi^*_{n'}(S) &= c(S) - c\left(S - \{n\}\right) + c(S) - c\left(S - \{n'\}\right) \\ &> c(S) - c\left(S - \{n, n'\}\right),\end{aligned}$$

and by equation (12) we conclude that $\pi^*(S) \notin core\left(S \cup \{0\}, c\right)$. ■

In order to prove proposition 3.8, we will make use of each bidder's indirect utility function, defined for a vector of prices $p \in \mathbb{R}^L_+$ as $u_n(p) = \max_{x_n} p \cdot x_n - C(x_n, \theta_n)$. Next, we will state three lemmas that trace the main steps of the proof. Lemmas will be proved later.

Lemma 3.9

The function $u_n(p)$ is nondecreasing. Further, if goods are substitutes in seller n's cost function, u_n has *decreasing differences*: for all i, $p_{-i} \geq p'_{-i}$, $u_n(p_i, p_{-i}) - u_n(p_i, p'_{-i})$ is nonincreasing in p_i.

Lemma 3.10

The coalition-value function satisfies $c(S) = \min_p u_S(p) - p \cdot \overline{x}$.

Lemma 3.11

The indirect utility function of coalition S satisfies $u_S(p) = \Sigma_{n \in S} u_n(p)$.

Proof of Proposition 3.8

Take any pair of prices $p^1 = (p_1^1, \ldots, p_L^1)$, $p^2 = (p_1^2, \ldots, p_L^2) \in \mathbb{R}_+^L$ and define $p^U \overset{\text{def}}{=} \left(\max\{p_1^1, p_1^2\}, \ldots, \max\{p_L^1, p_L^2\}\right)$ and $p^L \overset{\text{def}}{=} \left(\min\{p_1^1, p_1^2\}, \ldots, \min\{p_L^1, p_L^2\}\right)$. For any two bidders $n, n' \in S$, we have:

$$\begin{aligned}
c(S) + c\left(S - \{n, n'\}\right) &\leq \left(u_s(p^L) - p^L \cdot \overline{x}\right) \\
&+ \left(u_{S-\{n,n'\}}(p^U) - p^U \cdot \overline{x}\right) \leq \sum_{k \in S} u_k\left(p^L\right) \\
&+ \sum_{k \in S - \{n, n'\}} u_k(p^U) - (p^U + p^L) \cdot \overline{x} = u_n(p^L) + u_{n'}(p^L) \\
&+ \sum_{k \in S - \{n, n'\}} \left(u_k(p^U) + u_k(p^L)\right) - (p^U + p^L) \cdot \overline{x}.
\end{aligned}$$

The first inequality comes from lemma 3.10 and the second from lemma 3.11. Next, lemma 3.9 tells us that for every k, u_k is nondecreasing and has decreasing differences. So:

$$\begin{aligned}
c(S) + c\left(S - \{n, n'\}\right) &\leq u_n(p^1) + u_{n'}(p^2) \\
&+ \sum_{k \in S - \{n, n'\}} \left(u_k(p^1) + u_k(p^2)\right) - (p^U + p^L)\overline{x}. \\
&= \left(\sum_{k \in S - \{n'\}} u_k(p^1) - p^1 \cdot \overline{x} \right) + \left(\sum_{k \in S - \{n\}} u_k(p^2) - p^2 \cdot \overline{x} \right).
\end{aligned}$$

The last line used the fact that $p^L + p^U = p^1 + p^2$. Minimizing the last expression over (p^1, p^2) results in $c(S) + c(S - \{n, n'\}) \leq c(S - \{n\}) + c(S - \{n'\})$. Thus, coalition values are bidder submodular. ■

Proof of Lemma 3.9

By an envelope theorem (Milgrom and Segal, 2002), we know u_n is continuous everywhere and is differentiable at those prices with a single-valued solution. Further, $\frac{\partial u_n(p)}{\partial p_i} = x_{ni}(p)$, where $x_{ni}(p)$ is the quantity of good i supplied at price p. Then, u_n is nondecreasing. The substitutes condition is satisfied in the cost function if and only if $x_{ni}(p)$ is nonincreasing in each p_j for $j \neq i$. Thus, the substitutes property implies $\frac{\partial u_n(p)}{\partial p_i}$ is nonincreasing in each p_j for $j \neq i$, that is, u_n has decreasing differences. ■

Proof of Lemma 3.10

As defined earlier, the coalition-value function for a coalition S that includes the buyer with a demand vector z is given by $c(S,z) = \max_{\{x_1,\ldots,x_S\}, \Sigma x_n \leq z} P \cdot \left(\Sigma_{n \in S} x_n - z \right) - \Sigma_{n \in S} C(x_n, \theta_n)$, and the indirect utility function is given by $u_S(p) = \max_z p \cdot z + c(S, z)$. This means that $c(S, \overline{x}) \leq u_S(p) - p \cdot \overline{x}$ for all $p \in \mathbb{R}_+^L$. Let B be a large number that exceeds the incremental value of any good to any coalition. Further, by selecting p^* as $p_i^* = 0$, if $\overline{x}_i = 1$ and $p_i^* = B$ otherwise, we can achieve $u_S(p^*) = p^* \cdot \overline{x} + c(S, \overline{x})$. Then, $c(S, \overline{x}) = \min_p u_S(p) - p \cdot \overline{x}$. ■

Proof of Lemma 3.11

We just need to expand

$$u_S(p) = \max_z \{p \cdot z + c(S, z)\} = \max_z \Big\{p \cdot z + \max_{\{x_1, \ldots, x_S\}, \Sigma x_n \leq z} \times \{P \cdot (\Sigma_{n \in S} x_n - z) - \Sigma_{n \in S} C(x_n, \theta_n)\}\Big\} = \max_{\{x_1, \ldots, x_S\}} \times \Big\{P \cdot (\Sigma_{n \in S} x_n - z) + p \cdot \Sigma_{n \in S} x_n - \Sigma_{n \in S} C(x_n, \theta_n)\Big\} = \Sigma_{n \in S} u_n(p). \blacksquare$$

3.7 ADDITIONAL DRAWBACKS OF THE VICKREY AUCTION

We have already observed that one drawback of the Vickrey auction is that it can, in some examples, lead to low payoffs for the auctioneer. This means that the auctioneer incurs high costs if it is a buyer and/or low revenue if it is a seller. Other related drawbacks are reported in Ausubel and Milgrom (2006). Here, we consider some drawbacks that have received relatively less attention.

3.7.1 REPORTING COMPLEXITY

In a Vickrey auction, each bidder is required to report bids for each combination of items that it may be assigned. In an auction with N items, there are 2^N possible combinations—a number that quickly becomes unwieldy as N increases.

Sometimes, it is nevertheless possible to run a practical sealed-bid auction in a situation like that by using a compact language to express preferences. We do not develop the theory of bidding languages here. Interested readers should refer to Hatfield and Milgrom (2005) and Milgrom (2009) for bidding languages that represent substitutes preferences and to Eilat and Milgrom (2011) for a compact language to express preferences that include limited complementarities.

3.7.2 COMPUTATIONAL COMPLEXITY

A second drawback of the Vickrey auction is that the computations it requires may be impossible for some applications. First, just computing the Vickrey outcome $x_0^*(\theta)$ requires solving an optimization problem. When the choices are discrete and the goods are not substitutes, optimization can be very hard. In such cases, computing a Vickrey price for each winner m according to formula (8) requires a second optimization to determine $\pi_{-m}(\theta_{-m})$.

When exact computations are impossible, might an auction that determines assignments and prices by substituting approximate optimization into the Vickrey formulas work almost as well as a Vickrey auction? In the large problems for which optimization fails, the answer is often "no." For example, consider an auction with a large number of bidders N in which some more or less fixed fraction represents winners. The value of the optimum grows in proportion to N, but the price to be paid to each winning bidder stays roughly constant. So, a 1 percent error in estimating the optimum value with a bidder omitted corresponds to an N% pricing error. The same idea applies to any error of fixed size. Even with a pretty good approximate optimization, the errors in estimating Vickrey prices grow unacceptably large as the problem grows large.

This is another case in which the substitutes condition can be helpful, because an algorithm mimicking the Kelso-Crawford model in chapter 2 can quickly compute stable (and hence efficient) allocations when goods are substitutes.

3.7.3 BIDDERS WITH FINANCIAL CONSTRAINTS

In our model of the Vickrey auction, we have assumed that bidders are sellers and that the case of buyers is symmetric. This is true in the simplest models, but financial constraints can operate differently for buyers and sellers and can upset conclusions about strategy-proofness. So, for this subsection only, let us assume that the bidders are buyers and consider the problem of a bidder who can buy one or two units of a good. By putting one unit to work, the bidder can earn a profit of ten; by putting two units to work, a profit of twenty. The lender, however, is willing to lend just ten to participate in the auction. If the bidder cannot bid more than ten for any package of items, how should he or she bid? It is always best to bid ten for the package of two items, but how much should be bid for just one item? The important conclusion is that the answer depends on how others bid: the bidder has no dominant strategy.

To see that, suppose there is just one competing bidder. We consider two cases. In the first, the competitor bids five for one unit and makes no bid for two units. In that case, the first bidder's best outcome is to acquire two units for a price of five. He or she can achieve that only by bidding *less than five* for a single unit. In the second case, however, the competitor bids twelve for one unit and eighteen for two units. Then, the first bidder's best outcome is to acquire one unit for a price of six, which can only be done by bidding *more than six* for one unit. The requirements of the two best responses are incompatible, so the bidder has no dominant strategy.

Financial constraints can affect sellers as well, if the seller is unable to finance certain profitable projects unless he or she receives a sufficiently high price. This can support examples similar to the preceding example, in which bidders were buyers.

3.7.4 UNDERSTANDING THE RULES

An important issue in practical auction design is to establish rules that bidders can understand and that attract them to participate. From that perspective, an important drawback of the Vickrey auction is that the prices can be quite hard to explain or, as explained earlier, even to compute or verify. This problem, however, is not limited to computationally complex auctions. Even in second-price auctions for a single item, human bidders in laboratory experiments frequently fail to bid according to their dominant strategies (Kagel et al., 1987; Kagel and Levin, 1993; Li, 2015). It can be difficult to explain rules to bidders: in experiments, bidders may continue to play dominated strategies in the second-price auction even after the dominance is explained to them. The logic of optimal bidding in Vickrey auctions can be difficult to understand and becomes even more difficult in more general settings.

3.7.5 JOINT DEVIATIONS

Finally, Vickrey auctions are vulnerable to profitable joint deviations—even by losing bidders. For example, suppose that the buyer can buy either from seller 1 or from sellers 2 and 3 and that the buyer's value from acquiring what it needs is one hundred in both cases. Suppose that seller 1 has a cost of fifteen of supplying its good and seller 2 and seller 3 each has a cost of ten. The Vickrey outcome is that seller 1 wins and receives a price of twenty.

What would happen in this situation if the losing sellers 2 and 3 colluded, making an agreement to bid X and Y, respectively? If $X+Y<15$, then the two colluders would win the Vickrey auction and receive prices of $15-Y$ and $15-X$, respectively. For example, if $X=Y=1$, then colluders would win and each receive a price of fourteen: quite a deal for them, though not for the buyer! Notice that this deal strictly increases the payoffs of the colluding bidders without actually requiring that either one make a payment to the other. Profitable collusion that requires cash transfers can leave a discoverable money trail that discourages such deals. Collusion that works without transfers, however, is much harder to detect and prove. The possibility of this sort of collusion is a potential weakness of the Vickrey mechanism, the importance of which needs to be evaluated in any real application.

3.7.6 VALUE PRIVACY

A final problem is that Vickrey auctions ask bidders for so much confidential information. Bidders may resist Vickrey auctions because bidder valuations are often highly confidential (Rothkopf et al., 1990). The reason is that their reports may affect more than just the auction prices; they may be used by workers, suppliers, and partners in subsequent negotiations to extract better terms from the bidder.

3.8 SUMMARY

Vickrey auctions have long been studied in economics because of their remarkable properties.

- The Vickrey auction makes truthful reporting optimal for bidders and selects value-maximizing allocation.
- The Vickrey auction is the only auction mechanism with those two properties.
- When goods are substitutes, the Vickrey payments lead to outcomes in the core, which we have shown means that they are competitive in a reasonable sense.
- However, there are examples in which Vickrey payments lead to outcomes that are not in the core. Such outcomes always involve a strictly lower payoff for the auctioneer than any core allocation and a weakly higher payoff for every bidder than any core allocation.
- When a single bidder-seller makes an investment, the same choice that maximizes the total payoff to all participants also maximizes the single bidder's payoff.
- When there are multiple bidder-sellers that can invest to reduce their costs, there is a Nash equilibrium of the investment game, in which every seller invests efficiently.

- However, there can be other pure Nash equilibria with inefficient investments, either because the level of investment is wrong (too low or too high) or because the wrong bidders invest.
- Despite their advantages, Vickrey auctions also have several potentially important drawbacks:
  - The auctioneer's Vickrey payoff can be very low, even when there are losing bidders who are willing to offer a better deal.
  - In a sealed-bid mechanism, the bidder potentially has to name values for a large number of combinations, which can be daunting.
  - Vickrey auctions have no dominant strategy property in situations in which bidders are subject to financial constraints (such as credit or budget constraints) that limit the amounts they can bid.
  - Computing the allocation in a Vickrey auction requires solving an optimization, which can be challenging in some settings. Computing the price for each winning bidder requires solving another optimization, so with k winners, the auctioneers must solve $k+1$ optimizations. In practice, these computations can make the Vickrey auction hard for bidders to understand, potentially leading them to play dominated strategies or discouraging them from bidding at all.
  - In a Vickrey auction, losing bidders can sometimes collude profitably to become winning bidders. Moreover, that collusion can be strictly profitable for all the parties involved, with no need for colluders to make potentially detectable cash transfers among themselves.

- Vickrey auctions require bidders to report values honestly, but bidders may want to conceal that information because of effects it may have on future negotiations. This motive can ruin the mechanism's truthful reporting property.

4

DEFERRED-ACCEPTANCE AUCTIONS AND NEAR-SUBSTITUTES

Vickrey auctions are the only strategy-proof direct mechanisms that compute and select efficient allocations. Despite this considerable advantage, some of the disadvantages of Vickrey auctions listed at the end of chapter 3 are so severe as to make that design impractical or unacceptable for some applications.

Complex constraints can pose a difficult challenge for the Vickrey auction. In this chapter, I describe the challenge in the context of the FCC broadcast incentive auction, because of its size and economic significance. In that application, the greatest number of constraints were associated with ensuring that no two TV stations broadcast in a way that causes unacceptable interference. Similar pairwise constraints are found in many applications, particularly in transportation systems. For example, in air traffic control, flights need to be scheduled so that no two aircraft get too close, and a similar restriction applies to rail transportation.

For the FCC broadcast incentive auction, the problem of computing optimal allocations was so intractable as to sink a proposal to use a Vickrey auction. Simulations on the problem showed that even weeks of computing with fast computers using the best commercially available algorithms (Gurobi and C-Plex) applied to careful problem formulations could not find the optimum. Given the problem difficulty, the analysts did well by finding a solution that delivered at least 97 percent of the optimum, but that is not nearly good enough to compute even a decent approximation to Vickrey prices.

Here is the reason: for each station n that is a winning bidder, the exact Vickrey price is $\hat{V}_n - \bar{V} + v_n$, where $\bar{V}$ is the maximum total value of the stations left on the air when n is allowed to be a winner, and $\hat{V}_n$ is the maximum total value when station n is constrained to be a loser. To see how serious the estimation problem can be, suppose that one of these computations, say $\hat{V}_n$, could be done exactly, while the other was just 0.99 times the actual optimum, that is, $0.99\bar{V}$. Then, the estimated Vickrey price paid to a winner would then be too high by $.01\bar{V}$. With about two thousand TV broadcast stations in the United States, the average station value must be about $.0005\bar{V}$, so the Vickrey pricing error is about twenty times the average station value. If the estimation errors were reversed, the error magnitude would remain the same but the estimated Vickrey price would usually be negative, in violation of the logic of the Vickrey auction. What this analysis shows is that even just to get a reasonable estimate of the Vickrey prices, the maximization would need to be very nearly perfect. That is a problem for this application, because verifying the correctness of the Vickrey price computation is an NP-complete problem. With thousands of choice variables and 2.7 million constraints, the incentive auction is much too large to ensure computations of the accuracy that this problem requires.

What can be done? At a minimum, the computational issues imply that auction design needs to give up on the goal of achieving an actual optimum, but that still leaves challenges. First, we would like any algorithm we use to deliver a high fraction of the possible value, so that not too much is lost on account of failures of optimality. Second, once we give up on optimality, that may enable the auction to have other good properties that the Vickrey auction lacks. We might hope for better incentive properties (such as some sort of group strategy-proofness), greater simplicity (computations that are more obvious for bidders), or greater privacy preservation for winning bidders about how much they would be willing to pay. The final auction design, based on the theory presented in this chapter, delivers all of these advantages.

4.1 ALTERNATIVES TO THE VICKREY AUCTION

Much of the theory described in this chapter was initially created to deal with the special challenges of the FCC broadcast "incentive auction."

4.1.1 THE INCENTIVE AUCTION PROJECT

As described in chapter 1, the television industry has revolutionized itself several times since the mid-twentieth century. Initially, everyone who watched television saw over-the-air broadcast on one of the three VHF ("very high frequency") channels, which were channels 2, 4, and 7. Gradually, more channels became available, including ones in the UHF ("ultra-high frequency") range, which were considered inferior for the analog TV signals of the early era. Next came cable and satellite television, and then the transition from analog signals to digital ones, which made much more efficient use of the available frequencies, allowing high-definition programming.

By 2012, about 90 percent of U.S. homes were receiving their TV signals using cable or satellite, rather than over-the-air broadcasting. In the five years from 2007 (when the first iPhone was introduced) to 2012, there had been explosive growth in the demand for frequencies to use for mobile Internet access, and that growth was forecast to continue. Policy makers wondered whether they could enable a swap, in which the frequencies used for UHF-TV broadcast might be bought by mobile phone companies and others, who found these frequencies to be ideal ones for fourth-generation mobile broadband technologies. The incentive auction is an attempt to enable such a swap and at the same time to raise money for the U.S. Treasury.

The incentive auction is historic for several reasons. First, the amounts of money at stake are extremely high, potentially involving tens of billions of dollars. Second, there had never been such a swap in an auction before. Earlier spectrum auctions sold rights to use frequencies that were currently unused, so they did not need to worry about whether sufficient money could be raised to pay the sellers. The most novel and difficult parts of the auction design were related to buying television spectrum from UHF broadcasters that would be sufficient to clear a certain number of channels and make them available for other uses.

4.1.2 ALLOCATION CONSTRAINTS IN THE FCC BROADCAST INCENTIVE AUCTION

The first task in describing the auction in formal terms is to develop notation to describe the assignment of stations to channels. The variables we will define are logical variables, that is, statements about the assignment. We will write (X, c) to mean that "station X is assigned to broadcast on channel c." This is just a statement, so it can be true or false. An assignment of TV stations to channels is a set of true statements, that is, a set of pairs $P \subseteq S \times C$, where S is the set of stations and C is the set of possible channels.

Certain combinations of statements cannot be simultaneously true, either for logical reasons or because the proposed station assignment would create unacceptable interference between broadcasters. For example, two stations broadcasting from nearby towers cannot both use the same channel. All the constraints for this problem involve either a single station or a pair of stations.

To describe the logical constraints, I use $\neg$ to denote logical "not," $\vee$ to denote logical "or," and $\wedge$ to denote logical "and." The constraints are described by a collection of sets $(C_X, X \in S)$ and a set $\hat{I}$, with the interpretation that $C_X \subseteq C$ is the subset of channels to which station X is allowed to be assigned and $\hat{I} \subseteq (X \times C)^2$ lists all the incompatible channel assignments for pairs of stations. With those interpretations, the constraints, stated both in English and in mathematical notation, look like this:

1. "Every station X in S is assigned to (at least) one of its eligible channels."

$$\wedge_{X \in S} \vee_{c \in C_x} (X, c)$$

2. "No station in S is assigned to two different channels."

$$\wedge_{X \in S} \wedge_{c \neq c' \in C} \left(\neg(X, c) \vee \neg(X, c') \right)$$

3. "No two stations are assigned to channels in an incompatible way."

$$\wedge_{(X, c, X', c') \in \hat{I}} \left(\neg(X, c) \vee \neg(X', c') \right)$$

For the FCC broadcast incentive auction, there are about 2.7 million such constraints. It is simplest to say that two stations located close together cannot be assigned to the same channel.

To gain some insight into the problem, let us focus on the special case in which two conditions apply. The first is that all stations are eligible to use the same channels C, allowing us to replace C_X by C in the logical constraints. The second is that the *only* relevant interference is between two stations in close proximity. When these conditions are satisfied, we can write the constraints more simply using a graph, in the following way.

Let $A \subseteq S \times S$ describe the set of pairs of stations that are too close together to be assigned to the same channel. Our assumptions mean that $\hat{I}=\{(X,c,X',c)| c\in C,(X,X')\in A\}$. I treat the stations S as nodes in a graph and I treat A as a corresponding set of *arcs*. Two stations $(X,X')\in A$ are said to be *adjacent*. Checking whether it is feasible to assign channels to stations in a noninterfering way using just $|C|$ channels has the same logical structure as the *graph-coloring problem* of deciding, for the given graph (S,A), whether it is possible, using $|C|$ colors, to color each node such that no two adjacent nodes are the same color.

This graph-coloring problem is known to be NP-complete (Karp, 1975). For every known algorithm for any NP-complete class of problems, there is a series of problems of size s in the class of size for which the solution time grows exponentially in s. In practice, this means that for problems of moderate size, there are some that take a very long time to solve, even on the fastest computers.

This computational complexity is important for applications like the incentive auction, in which TV stations that do not sell their rights must be assigned to some channel. To determine whether it is possible to accept one set of bids by TV stations and to reject the bids of others, the FCC must determine whether there is any feasible way to assign channels to the stations that do not sell. As we have seen, this is quite similar to a graph-coloring problem, and it can be very hard.

4.1.3 SINGLE-MINDED BIDDERS

Throughout this chapter, we will limit our attention to "single-minded seller-bidders," meaning bidders who have only one station to sell and whose single decision is to sell or not. Some bidders in the actual incentive auction owned multiple stations, and some had additional options for the stations beyond selling or not, so the theory developed here is not a perfect fit for the application. If TV stations that were part of a large group tended to be the ones with higher values, then most of the actual sellers in the auction would be single-minded bidders. For most of these smaller bidders, selling or not selling were the main options, and in that case mitigating the bidding problem facing these bidders would be the central design challenge.[1]

One particular need for smaller bidders was to ensure that they could understand the auction rules and the incentives implied by those rules. The computations needed to be much simpler than those of the Vickrey auction, which are so difficult and opaque that, even if the technical experts could actually find a way to perform them, the bidders might not trust their correctness. The consequences of bidder disbelief could be nonparticipation, threatening the success of the auction.

4.1.4 "OBVIOUSLY STRATEGY-PROOF" MECHANISMS: INFORMAL DISCUSSION

Strategy-proof mechanisms can have important advantages over other kinds of mechanisms, because bidding is easy and certain costs are saved. In our theoretical model, a bidder who learns about its competitors' bids cannot use that information to bid smarter, because simple, truthful bidding is always optimal. No bidder can improve its chances by studying or spying on competitors to learn their types or by encrypting its information to conceal its type. In contrast to a standard sealed tender, in which a bidder might hope to surprise a competitor to win an item for a bargain price, there is no such potential gain in a strategy-proof auction.

Yet even strategy-proofness may not be enough to make bidding truly simple for human bidders. We have already seen that strategy-proof Vickrey auctions may encounter severe computational issues, but even when they do not, the advantages of a strategy-proof mechanism may not be fully realized, for several reasons. First, experimental evidence (Kagel and Levin, 1993) suggests that bidders in ordinary second-price auctions often make mistakes, despite the fact that the mechanism is strategy-proof. Second, in settings in which computations are challenging, it may be hard to convince bidders about strategy-proofness. Third, if bidders cannot verify the computations, they may doubt the auctioneer's ability to do those computations correctly. Finally, bidders may worry that a dishonest auctioneer might peek at the bids and submit additional, losing bids to manipulate the auction prices.

All these problems can be overcome by abandoning any direct mechanism in favor of a more dynamic auction mechanism to create a strategy-proof mechanism that a bidder can believe in, even if the bidder does not understand the computations required by the outcome function, does not trust the auctioneer to compute it correctly, cannot reason about strategy-proofness along the lines of the proof of proposition 2.7, and does not trust the auctioneer not to peek at the bids that the sellers make. In the words of Shengwu Li (2015), such a mechanism is "obviously strategy-proof." A hint that this is possible comes from the other finding of Kagel and Levin (1993), which is that in the same laboratory setting in which bidders are confused by a second-price auction, they nevertheless play their dominant truthful strategies in a simple ascending auction of the type used on eBay.

Unlike a direct mechanism, a *dynamic mechanism* is one in which some participant does not merely report values but may instead have multiple opportunities to act. For example, in an ascending auction, a bidder typically gets multiple opportunities to improve (that is, raise) its bid. If the bidders are sellers, then a descending auction works similarly, in which bidders may dynamically improve their offers by reducing their bids.

In a dynamic mechanism, a strategy σ_n^* (the "truthful" strategy) for bidder n is said to be *obviously dominant* (according to Li's definition) if for any other strategy σ_n for the same bidder, at any choice node for n where the two strategies first diverge, the *highest possible payoff* from continuing to follow σ_n is less than or equal to the *lowest possible payoff* from continuing to follow σ_n^*. If a mechanism has the property that each bidder always has an obviously dominant strategy, then the mechanism is *obviously strategy-proof.* We give only a verbal account of this concept in this section, using formal notation for a specific class of auctions in the next section.[2]

When the auctioneer has a single object to sell (or buy), it is easy to see that Vickrey's second-price auction is *not* obviously strategy-proof. For suppose some bidder is willing to sell the item he or she values at ten and considers whether to bid eight instead. If the bidder bids ten, the dominant strategy, the worst that can happen is that he or she might lose, earning a payoff of zero. If the bidder instead bids eight, he or she might win at a price $X > 10$, earning a positive payoff in case $X - 10 > 0$, so the best possible payoff is strictly positive. Since the lowest payoff from truthful bidding is less than the best payoff from the deviation, the auction is obviously not strategy-proof.

In contrast, consider a dynamic clock auction mechanism, wherein "clock" is the informal name for a display that shows a price that may change. The price clock starts high and ticks down during the auction. Whenever a bidder's price changes, the bidder is asked whether he or she wants to remain active. If a bidder ever answers "no," then that bidder exits the auction. When there is just one remaining bidder who has never said "no," that bidder wins and pays the last price that he or she had accepted. With very small decrements (smaller than any difference between the bidders' costs of supply), if the prices displayed to bidders are nearly equal, with only one bidder's price adjusted at a time, then this mechanism mimics the Vickrey auction. The reasons are, first, that this mechanism is strategy-proof, second, that the last bidder to remain active is the one with the lowest cost of supply, and third, that the clock price at that time is nearly equal to the second-lowest cost of supply.

Unlike the Vickrey auction, in this clock auction each bidder has an *obviously* dominant strategy: he or she should say "yes" as long as the price is greater than his or her value, and otherwise he or she should say "no." To confirm that this "truthful" strategy is obviously dominant, notice that starting at any choice node, the bidder can never sell the good at a loss, so the *lowest possible continuation payoff from truthful bidding is zero*. If the bidder adopts any other strategy, then starting from any choice node where that strategy deviates from the truthful strategy, the *highest possible continuation payoff is zero*. The reason is that such a bidder either deviates to say "no," which always pays zero, or deviates to say "yes" when the price is already below his or her value, in which case the best that can happen is that he or she loses and earns zero.

There is a lot of subtlety packed into the definition of obvious strategy-proofness. First, compared with checking for dominant strategies, it may be easier for a bidder to check during the play of the mechanism whether a proposed strategy is obviously dominant, because checking requires comparing just two numbers representing a best-case payoff and a worst-case payoff, although this comparison needs to be made at each moment of choice. In contrast, in a second-price auction, to check that truthful bidding is better than any particular alternative strategy, the bidder would need to compute and compare two vectors of potential payoffs that correspond to what it might earn against all possible strategy combinations of the other bidders. To verify that a strategy is dominant, it must do that for every alternative strategy. In ordinary language, this is what is sometimes meant by saying that verifying dominance in the Vickrey auction requires "contingent reasoning": the bidder needs to think through individual cases and compare what would happen in each case for the two strategies being compared. A mechanism that is obviously strategy-proof relieves participants of the need to use contingent reasoning.

Second, in the clock auction, the bidder's need to understand and trust the mechanism operator is reduced. To conclude that a strategy is obviously dominant, the bidder needs to know just two things: if it says "no," it will exit with a payoff of zero, and if it says "yes," it will either win the right to supply at that price or the mechanism will continue by naming another, lower price. Among the things that the bidder does *not* need to know are how many other bidders are participating, how many items are being purchased, what future prices the clock might select, and whether the clock can tick down even when no other bidders are still active. The bidder does not need to know or understand or trust anything more than the two things identified above to reach its conclusion. In addition, the bidder does not need to fear that the auctioneer will peek at its bid when it should not. The auctioneer routinely looks at the bids to operate the mechanism, but in contrast with a sealed-bid auction, in which it can then learn about how to manipulate prices safely, it has no safe manipulation in the clock auction, because it does not know how the bidder will respond to the next price.

Dynamics can help to simplify incentive calculations, but to compare the outcomes of dynamic mechanisms to those of other mechanisms, it is still helpful to work with direct mechanisms. Once we have specified the number of bidders, their truthful strategies, and the rules for when the clock ticks and by how much, if we are given the bidders' types θ, we can then infer the allocation and prices that would result from truthful bidding in the dynamic mechanism. Call the allocation-price pair $\left(\alpha(\theta), p^{\alpha}(\theta)\right)$. The mechanism that takes reports of bidders' types and produces the outcome

$\left(\alpha(\theta), p^{\alpha}(\theta)\right)$ is a direct mechanism. Clearly, if the dynamic auction is obviously strategy-proof, then (α, p^{α}) is a strategy-proof direct mechanism.

Intuitively, the direct mechanism describes a situation in which bidders report their types to the auctioneer, who promises to play the truthful strategy in the dynamic mechanism, just as the bidder would want. A bidder who finds it profitable to misrepresent its type to the auctioneer would have to find it profitable to deviate from obviously strategy-proof play, which is a contradiction.

4.2 DEFERRED-ACCEPTANCE CLOCK AUCTIONS

Let us now return to an environment in which the auctioneer is a buyer, the bidders are sellers, and each bidder has a single item to offer for sale. The clock auctions that we had described informally earlier involve an iterated process, during which bidders who reject a price are irreversibly removed from the auction, but no bidder is accepted as a winner until the very end of the auction. The facts that acceptance decisions are deferred until the end and that this characteristic is shared with the famous Gale-Shapley deferred-acceptance algorithm lead us to call these *deferred-acceptance clock auctions.*[3]

To put enough detail into our previous informal description to allow a formal treatment, two additional specifications are needed. The first of these concerns what each bidder is told during the auction about what has happened so far, and the second is the specification of how the price offers are determined. In any strategy-proof mechanism, participants' optimal choices remain optimal regardless of what they learn about their competitors' moves, so we can simplify our description by limiting attention to mechanisms in which bidders are told the whole past history of play when they make their decisions. In the next paragraph, the only formal distinction that we make among different deferred-acceptance clock auctions is the different functions p that they use to determine how prices are set. The only restriction we will place on p is that no bidder's price can ever increase from one round to the next.

The key concepts for which we need to introduce notation are those of rounds, active bidders, and histories. The auction takes place in a discrete series of rounds, $t = 1, 2, \ldots$, and in each round t, some set of bidders $A_t \subseteq \mathcal{N}$ is still "active." The history of activity in the auction through round t is denoted $A^t \stackrel{\text{def}}{=} (A_1, \ldots, A_t)$. Let $\mathcal{H}$ be the set of all possible histories of activity.

A clock auction is a function $p : \mathcal{H} \to \mathbb{R}_+^N$ such that for all $t \geq 2$ and all histories A^t, $p(A^t) \leq p(A^{t-1})$. The function p identifies an *economic mechanism* that is played as follows. Initially, all bidders are active: $A_1 = \mathcal{N}$; and the prices offered at round 1 are given by the vector $p(A_1) = p(\mathcal{N})$. In every round t, the prices are given by the vector $p(A^t)$, and each bidder n is informed of the whole history A^t. Each bidder n for whom $p_n(A^t) < p_n(A^{t-1})$ then makes a binary choice about whether to *exit*, while bidders for whom $p_n(A^t) = p_n(A^{t-1})$ make no choice. A bidder who does not exit is said to *continue*. The set of bidders who choose to exit at round t are denoted by $E_t \subseteq A_t$. The active bidders in the next round are those who have not exited: $A_{t+1} = A_t - E_t$.

By construction, the prices offered to any bidder n in successive rounds $t-1$ and t can only decrease: $p_n(A^t) \leq p_n(A^{t-1})$. The auction ends at the first round $t \geq 2$ for which $p(A^t) = p(A^{t-1})$, that is, the auction ends when the pricing rule specifies that the prices do not change. In the final round t, bidder n is a winner if and only if $n \in A_t$. A winning bidder n sells its good and is paid the final price $p_n(A^t)$. Translated into words, this means the winning bidders are those who are still active at the end of the auction, and the price paid is the final clock price.

Let $\mathcal{H}_n = \left\{A^t \in \mathcal{H} \mid p_n(A^t) < p_n(A^{t-1})\right\}$. Those are the histories at which n must make a choice to exit or not. Bidder n's plan for play in this mechanism is called a *strategy* and is a function $\sigma_n : \mathcal{H}_n \to \{exit, continue\}$. That is, a strategy specifies whether to exit after any history of play. If T is the final round of the auction, then the final history is denoted by $A^T(\sigma)$, and each bidder n's payoff is described by:

$$\pi_n\left(A^T(\sigma)\right) = \begin{cases} 0 & \text{if } n \notin A^T(\sigma) \\ p_n\left(A^T(\sigma)\right) - v_n & \text{if } n \in A^T(\sigma) \end{cases}, \quad (13)$$

where v_n is the bidder's (opportunity) cost of supplying its item. Bidders who are no longer active at the end of the auction are "losing bidders": they neither supply goods nor receive payments, and they earn zero payoffs. A bidder who is still active at the end becomes a winner, supplies an item, and receives a payoff equal to the difference between the price received and the cost of supply.

4.2.1 INCENTIVE PROPERTIES

Our first task is to characterize the especially good incentive properties of deferred-acceptance clock auctions. Two kinds of properties are treated here. One concerns obvious strategy-proofness, and the other concerns the incentives of groups of bidders to collude in the auction.

Definitions

1. A strategy profile $\sigma=(\sigma_1,\ldots,\sigma_N)$ is *consistent with history* A^t, which we write as $\sigma\in C(A^t)$, if the history A^t results at round t from the play of σ.
2. A strategy σ_n obviously dominates strategy $\hat{\sigma}_n$ if $\sigma_n(A^t)\neq\hat{\sigma}_n(A^t)$ implies that

$$\max_{\{\sigma_{-n}|(\hat{\sigma}_n,\sigma_{-n})\in C(A^t)\}}\pi_n\left(A^T(\hat{\sigma}_n,\sigma_{-n})\right)$$
$$\leq\min_{\{\sigma_{-n}|(\sigma_n,\sigma_{-n})\in C(A^t)\}}\pi_n\left(A^T(\hat{\sigma}_n,\sigma_{-n})\right).$$

3. A strategy σ_n is *obviously dominant* if it obviously dominates every alternative strategy $\hat{\sigma}_n$.
4. The truthful strategy in a deferred-acceptance clock auction specifies that $\sigma_n(A^t)=exit$ if $p_n(A^t)<v_n$ and $\sigma_n(A^t)=continue$ otherwise.

Intuitively, a strategy σ_n is obviously dominant if, after any possible history of play A^t, the best that it can hope to earn from an immediate deviation is no better than the worst that it can earn from never deviating and always playing according to σ_n. Proofs of obvious strategy-proofness should themselves be obvious—how else could a bidder understand?—and fortunately this one is.

Proposition 4.1

In every deferred-acceptance clock auction, the truthful strategy is obviously dominant.

Proof

Suppose first that $p_n(A^t) \geq v_n$. If a seller deviates from truthful bidding by exiting in that situation, then that exit implies that $n \notin A^T$: the bidder loses and earns a payoff of zero. Truthful bidding never involves a payoff less than zero, so truthful bidding is always at least as good as the best possibility along any continuation path of play when $p_n(A^t) \geq v_n$.

Next, suppose that $p_n(A^t) < v_n$. Then, a bidder bidding truthfully exits and earns a payoff of zero. If a seller deviates from truthful bidding in that situation, there are two possibilities. Either $n \notin A^T$ (the seller loses), in which case his or her payoff is zero; or $n \in A^T$, in which case he or she wins at a price $p_n(A^T) \leq p_n(A^t) < v_n$ and earns a payoff of $p_n(A^T) - v_n < 0$. The best possibility is that he or she earns zero, so truthful bidding is always at least as good as the best hoped-for possibility along any continuation path of play when $p_n(A^t) < v_n$. ■

One interesting implication of obvious strategy-proofness concerns the incentives for groups of bidders to collude. No auction is immune to collusion whereby the winners can bribe the losers to go away or to avoid competing fiercely.

But Vickrey auctions, as we have already seen, are even more susceptible than that. They do not require the payment of bribes to encourage collusion. Losers in such auctions can sometimes collude in ways that allow them to become profitable winners. That is potentially important, because collusion in the form of payments creates a much greater risk of detection than the sort of collusion that requires no such payments, but just a wink and a nod and a recognition of the bidders' mutual interests. So it is worth noting when an auction is resistant to that weaker form of collusion, that is, when there is no way for any group of bidders to change their strategies in the auction itself that leads all of them to get strictly higher payoffs.

Definition

An auction is *group strategy-proof* if (i) truthful bidding (denoted by $\bar{\sigma}$) is a dominant strategy and (ii) there is no set of bidders S and alternative strategy profile σ such that for all $n \in S$, $\pi_n(\sigma_S, \bar{\sigma}_{N-S}) > \pi_n(\bar{\sigma})$.

Proposition 4.2

Every deferred-acceptance clock auction is group strategy-proof.

Proof

Consider any set of potential colluders S' and consider the first round in which one of them, say bidder n, deviates from truthful bidding. At that point, its price is no higher than its value, so n's deviation can never lead to a payoff larger than zero, regardless of the strategies of the other players in S'. In comparison, truthful bidding never leads to a payoff of less than zero. So bidder n does not strictly profit from joining the collusive group. ■

4.2.2 DEFERRED-ACCEPTANCE CLOCK AUCTIONS AS GREEDY ALGORITHMS

Let us suppose again that the auctioneer/buyer has constraints that govern the set of bidders/sellers it can reject while still meeting its purchase objective. Our goal is to consider deferred-acceptance clock auctions that are guaranteed to satisfy the buyer's constraints.

Using the notation defined earlier, a set of bids A is acceptable to the buyer if $A \in \mathcal{A}$. The corresponding sets of bids that can feasibly be rejected are those in $\mathcal{R} = \{R \mid R^c \in \mathcal{A}\}$. We frame the problem by adopting the two properties of $\mathcal{R}$ described in chapter 3, namely, (1) $\emptyset \in \mathcal{R}$ and (2) $R' \subset R \in \mathcal{R} \Rightarrow R' \in \mathcal{R}$. The first property means that when all bidders are present at the start of the auction, the outcome of letting all be winners is feasible. The second property means that if it is feasible to reject a set of bidders R (and to accept the complementary set of bidders A), then it is also possible to reject any subset of R (and accept any superset of A).

We limit our attention to a subset of the deferred-acceptance clock auctions that guarantee a feasible outcome. Intuitively, these work as follows. In each round, the auction checks whether the exit of any active bidder risks infeasibility and, if so, labels that bidder as *essential*, meaning that its price will not be further reduced and the bidder will eventually become a winner. The remaining active bidders are *inessential*. In any round t, the auction reduces the price of just one inessential bidder $\left(\text{denoted } n^*(A^t)\right)$ by some decrement $\left(\Delta(A^t) \leq p_{n^*}(A^{t-1})\right)$. We assume that the process is finite.[4] This process continues iteratively until all active bidders are either essential or are quoted a price of zero. Then, there are no further price changes, and the auction ends.

Here is the same auction algorithm expressed in notation.

One-bidder-at-a-time price-decrementing algorithm

1. Let $F_t = \left\{n \in A_t | p_n(A^{t-1}) > 0, \mathcal{N} - A_t \cup \{n\} \in \mathcal{R}\right\}$. (This is the set of inessential bidders with positive prices after round $t-1$.)
2. If $F_t = \varnothing$, $p(A^t) = p(A^{t-1})$ and the auction ends. (The auction ends when it is not possible to reduce any bidder's price offer without risking that it may exit and lead to an infeasible allocation.)
3. If $F_t \neq \varnothing$, then (one bidder's price is decremented)

$$p_n(A^t) = \begin{cases} p_n(A^{t-1}) - \Delta(A^t) & \text{if } n = n^*(A^t) \\ p_n(A^{t-1}) & \text{if } n \in A_t \text{ and } n \neq n^*(A^t) \end{cases}.$$

Since a bidder can choose to exit only when his or her price is reduced and since a bidder's price is reduced only when exit does not result in an infeasible allocation, the outcome of a deferred-acceptance clock auction with such a pricing algorithm is always feasible.

Proposition 4.3

Every deferred-acceptance clock auction with a one-bidder-at-a-time price-decrementing algorithm terminates in a feasible allocation.

A particularly simple algorithm in this class is one for which (i) the decrement $\Delta(A^t)=\Delta$ is a positive constant, and (ii) $n^*(A^t)$ cycles through the eligible bidder indices $1,\dots,N$, skipping over bidders who are essential or inactive or whose price is zero. We call this a *standard clock auction with decrement* Δ. At any round during such an auction, any two inessential bidders either have the same clock price or prices that differ by exactly Δ.

Suppose that each bidder n plays his or her obviously dominant strategy in a standard clock auction. Then, if the decrement Δ is sufficiently small, the first bidder to exit will be the inessential bidder who first finds the price has fallen below his or her value, which is the bidder with the highest value if there is a unique such bidder, or otherwise one of the bidders with the same, highest value. Once that bidder exits, the set of essential bidders is recomputed and possibly enlarged. The next bidder to exit will again be the currently inessential bidder with the highest value. The set of winners in a standard clock auction is therefore just the same as if the bidders had reported their values truthfully to the auctioneer, who then applied a greedy rejection algorithm to determine which bidders to reject. We say "a" greedy rejection algorithm rather than "the" greedy rejection algorithm, because in the event that two or more bidders have the same value, the ordering of the bidders may affect which among them is rejected.

Proposition 4.4

Suppose that $\Delta < \min\{v_i - v_j \mid i, j \in \mathcal{N}, v_i \neq v_j\}$. Then a standard clock auction with decrement Δ rejects bidders in the same way as a greedy rejection algorithm.

Next, we connect these results to matroids, as introduced in subsection 2.4. Combining propositions 4.4 and 2.14 leads to the following:

Proposition 4.5

If $\mathcal{R}$ is a matroid and $\Delta < \min\{v_i - v_j \mid i, j \in \mathcal{N}, v_i \neq v_j\}$, then a standard clock auction with decrement Δ results in an optimal allocation.

4.2.3 PRIVACY PROPERTIES

In a practical auction, there can be multiple reasons that either the auctioneer or a winning bidder might not want others to know what price the bidder would have been willing to accept. For the auctioneer, there is the risk that the public or its client may learn that the winning bidder in the reverse auction would have been willing to accept a much lower price. A famous example of such a problem in a forward auction came during a sale of television licenses in New Zealand in the 1980s. The government used a second-price auction, in which the winning bidder paid a price equal to the second-highest bid. In that particular auction, the winning bid was NZ$100,000, but the bidder paid only NZ$6, because that was the second-highest bid. (At the time NZ$1 = US$0.55.) Newspapers highlighted the huge discrepancy, embarrassing the government.

Bidders, too, may wish to conceal the prices they are willing to pay, in order that competitors, suppliers, and others will not know how profitable the particular deal might be.

In view of the common desire for privacy, another particularly nice property of descending clock auctions is that instead of requiring all bidders to reveal their exact values through their bids, it only requires winners to reveal the minimal information needed to prove that they should be winning. In computer science, the property is known as "unconditional privacy." Aside from alleviating bidders' concerns about revealing their values, this notion of privacy is also useful because it makes bidding easier for bidders who find it costly to figure out their exact values. Milgrom and Segal (2015) show that clock auctions are essentially the only mechanisms that provide dominant strategy incentives and also preserve winners' unconditional privacy.

4.3 APPROXIMATE MATROIDS AND THE SUBSTITUTABILITY INDEX

In practice, procedures based on greedy algorithms often perform very well. In small-scale simulations of the U.S. incentive auction conducted by Kevin Leyton-Brown, Neil

Newman, Ilya Segal, and me (Leyton-Brown et al., 2016), we found that the value achieved by the auction is typically more than 95 percent of the value achieved by an optimization. In the actual auction, Vickrey outcomes and prices cannot be computed at all. In our small-scale simulations, Vickrey outcomes took three orders of magnitude more time than the auction based on the greedy algorithm, but the latter achieved more than 95 percent of the value of the optimization. This surprisingly good performance calls for an explanation, and what I offer here is just an initial thought about where the explanation may lie.

Given the simplicity and good performance of a standard clock auction when $\mathcal{R}$ is a matroid, one might hope that some similar auction can perform well when the *relevant* part of the feasible set is *nearly* described by a matroid. To make formal sense of this claim, I need to give a formal account that adequately captures the meaning of the words "relevant" and "nearly."

Focusing first on the word "relevant," I have in mind problems like flight scheduling at a busy airport, in which the analyst might know or guess that some constraints, say runway space, are likely to be important determinants of the optimum, while other constraints, say terminal space, are less likely to be binding. To model that, suppose that the full set of constraints is described by a set $\mathcal{R}$ but that the analyst suspects that the optimum will lie in smaller $\mathcal{O} \subseteq \mathcal{R}$. Both $\mathcal{O}$ and $\mathcal{R}$ are assumed to have the free-disposal property. If the analyst has no useful information, that would be captured in the model by specifying that $\mathcal{O} = \mathcal{R}$. If the analyst knows that some constraints are sure to be binding and others are sure not to be binding, then it can happen that $\mathcal{O} \subset \mathcal{R}$.

For the word "nearly," I introduce an index to describe how well the sets in any particular matroid $\mathcal{M}$ approximates those in $\mathcal{O}$. Focusing on any particular set $X \in \mathcal{O}$, the best inner approximation is the set $M \in \mathcal{M}$ that contains the largest number of elements of X. I measure the worst-case quality of the approximation by $\min_{X \in \mathcal{O}} \max_{M \in \mathcal{M}, M \subseteq X} \frac{|M|}{|X|}$. I limit attention to approximating matroids $\mathcal{M} \subseteq \mathcal{R}$, so the approximating set $M \in \mathcal{M}$ is itself feasible. Given this approach, the ability to approximate the relevant constraints by a matroid is described by the "substitutability index," the definition of which follows.

Definition

Given a collection of subsets $\mathcal{R}$ of N, a *best approximating matroid* is denoted by $\mathcal{M}^* = \mathcal{M}^*(\mathcal{R}, \mathcal{O})$, and the *substitutability index* by $\rho(\mathcal{R}, \mathcal{O})$, where

$$\mathcal{M}^* \in argmax_{M \text{ a matroid}, M \subseteq R} \min_{X \in \mathcal{O}} \max_{M \in M, M \subseteq X} \frac{|M|}{|X|}, \quad (14)$$

and

$$\rho(\mathcal{R}, \mathcal{O}) \stackrel{\text{def}}{=} \min_{X \in \mathcal{O}} \max_{M \in \mathcal{M}^*, M \subseteq X} \frac{|M|}{|X|}. \quad (15)$$

If $\mathcal{R}$ is a matroid, then $\mathcal{M}^* = \mathcal{R}$ and $\rho(\mathcal{R}, \mathcal{O}) = 1$.

I show here that this index also describes the worst-case performance of a certain greedy algorithm in finding a near optimum, given the $\mathcal{R}$ and $\mathcal{O}$. Recall our notational convention: $v(S) \stackrel{\text{def}}{=} \Sigma_{n \in S} v_n$.

Proposition 4.6

$$\min_{v>0} \frac{\max_{M\in\mathcal{M}^*} v(M)}{\max_{S\in\mathcal{O}} v(S)} = \rho(\mathcal{R},\mathcal{O}).$$

Proof

Let

$$v^* \in argmin_{v>0} \frac{\max_{M\in\mathcal{M}^*} v(M)}{\max_{S\in\mathcal{O}} v(S)}, \rho^* \overset{\text{def}}{=} \frac{\max_{M\in\mathcal{M}^*} v^*(M)}{\max_{S\in\mathcal{O}} v^*(S)}.$$

Let $\underline{v} = \min\{v_n^* | v_n^* > 0\}$ and $X_+ = \{n | v_n^* = \underline{v}\}$. For $\alpha > 0$, define $\hat{v}_n^{*\alpha} \overset{\text{def}}{=} \begin{cases} \alpha\underline{v} & \text{if } n \in X_+ \\ v_n^* & \text{if } n \notin X_+ \end{cases}$. For α near 1, the corresponding value of the objective is given by the function:

$$\hat{\rho}(\alpha) \overset{\text{def}}{=} \frac{\max_{M\in\mathcal{M}^*} v^{*\alpha}(M)}{\max_{S\in\mathcal{O}} v^{*\alpha}(S)}$$

$$= \frac{\alpha\underline{v}|X_+ \cap X_{\mathcal{M}^*}| + \sum_{n\in(X_{\mathcal{M}^*}-X_+)\cap X_{\mathcal{M}^*}} v_n^*}{\alpha\underline{v}|X_+ \cap X_{\mathcal{O}}| + \sum_{n\in(X_{\mathcal{O}}-X_+)\cap X_{\mathcal{O}}} v_n^*},$$

where $X_{\mathcal{O}} \in argmax_{S\in\mathcal{O}} \Sigma_{n\in S} v_n^*$ and $X_{\mathcal{M}^*} \in argmax_{S\in\mathcal{M}^*} \Sigma_{n\in S} v_n^*$.

Notice that $\hat{\rho}(\cdot)$ is strictly monotonic unless $\rho^* = \frac{|X_+ \cap X_{\mathcal{M}^*}|}{|X_+ \cap X_{\mathcal{O}}|}$, and that by the optimality of $v^* = v^{*1}$, $\hat{\rho}(\alpha)$ is minimized at $\alpha = 1$. So $\rho^* = \frac{|X_+ \cap X_{\mathcal{M}^*}|}{|X_+ \cap X_{\mathcal{O}}|}$. Hence, $1_{X_+}, 1_{X_+ \cap X_{\mathcal{O}}} \in argmin_{v>0} \frac{\max_{M\in\mathcal{M}^*} v(M)}{\max_{S\in\mathcal{O}} v(S)}$, and so $\rho^* = \rho(\mathcal{R},\mathcal{O})$. ■

According to proposition 4.6, the substitutability index not only measures the worst-case proximity of sets but also the worst-case payoff ratio from solving the computationally easy problem on $\mathcal{M}^*$ instead of a computationally hard problem on $\mathcal{R}$. The problem on the matroid $\mathcal{M}^*$ is easy, because it is solved exactly by a greedy algorithm. Moreover, the greedy algorithm provides a monotonic winner selection rule, so it can be incorporated into a strategy-proof auction.

The significance of proposition 4.6 is greatest for applications like the broadcast incentive auction, in which the constraints are known in advance and there is some information about constraints that are likely to be binding at the optimum. The proposition implies that if $\rho(\mathcal{R}, \mathcal{O})$ is close to one, then it is possible to tailor a particular greedy algorithm that will work well for the actual constraints and for all values in some relevant set. The proposition gives a worst-case bound for performance of one particular greedy algorithm, which is the standard greedy algorithm but uses the constraints $\mathcal{M}^*$ instead of the actual constraints $\mathcal{R}$.

There are other greedy-like algorithms that perform even better than that. First, apply the standard greedy mechanism to $(N, v, \mathcal{M}^*)$. Then, when that stops, relax the constraints from $\mathcal{M}^*$ to $\mathcal{R}$ and pack additional items greedily so long as that is feasible. At worst, if no additional items can be packed, the solution is the same as for the approximating greedy algorithm. Often, however, this extension leads to a strict improvement, because it packs additional items. It is not hard to see that this improved greedy algorithm is still monotonic, so it can be used as part of a strategy-proof auction.

4.3.1 A CHANNEL ASSIGNMENT EXAMPLE

In the United States, as in most of the world, the major cities grew to take advantage of trade that came on ships. Consequently, for an approximation, we can conceptualize the cities and stations as being ordered linearly along a single shoreline, which we will assume is oriented from north to south. Suppose that within each metropolitan area, TV stations are close enough together that if two were to broadcast on the same channel, one would interfere with reception of the other for at least some customers. Suppose that, in addition, some stations near the boundaries of metropolitan areas could interfere with some stations in the next city, so those stations need to be assigned to different channels. Assume that there are C channels available, and that each station has a potential interference conflict only with its I nearest neighbors to the north and its I nearest neighbors to the south. Let $x(n)$ denote the city in which station n is located. An obvious necessary condition for a set of stations S to be feasible is that for each city X, $|\{n \in S | x(n) = X\}| \leq C$. This means that we cannot assign more stations in a city than the total number of available channels.

Given such a collection S, suppose that we try to assign channels to stations from north to south, starting with channel 1 and continuing through channel C, then starting over with channel 1 for the next station, and continuing in the same way. If $C > I$, then no station is assigned to the same channel as any of its I nearest neighbors to the north or south, so this assignment can never cause any interference. Hence, the feasible collections of stations $\mathcal{R}$ coincides with the matroid $\mathcal{R}'=\{S:|\{n\in S|x(n)=X\}|\le C\}$. If $C\le I$, it may still be possible to bound $\mathcal{R}$ from inside by a matroid $\mathcal{R}'$ created, for example, by adding the restriction that, in each city, no more than $C-1$ among the I northernmost stations can continue to broadcast and hence must be assigned channels. This extra constraint is not present in the actual problem, and adding it results in a matroid $\mathcal{R}'$ that is an inner bound for the actual constraint set $\mathcal{R}$, but a greedy algorithm run on this inner bound may nevertheless result in a good approximation of the optimum. Indeed, for that choice of $\mathcal{R}'$, $\min_{X\in\mathcal{R}}\max_{X'\in\mathcal{R}'}\frac{|X\cap X'|}{|X|}\ge\frac{C-1}{I}$. Thus, regardless of the actual values of the TV stations, a greedy algorithm using matroid $\mathcal{R}'$ selects a set of stations whose total value is at least $\frac{C-1}{I}$ of the optimum using the actual constraints.

4.4 INCENTIVE AUCTION CONSTRAINTS AND GREEDY ALGORITHMS

As in the preceding example, the constraints on the set of winning bidders in the FCC broadcast incentive auction are not given indirectly but as the solution to a second problem: that of finding a feasible way to assign TV channels to stations that allows them to broadcast over the air. In that second problem, there are two kinds of constraints. One directly limits the channels that are available for each broadcast station. For example, a station in Syracuse, New York, might be unable to use a particular channel, because that channel is reserved for use by a nearby Canadian station. The second kind of constraint forbids certain pairs of assignments. The most common instance of this constraint might forbid assigning two nearby stations, say stations X and Y, both to channel 26, either because their service areas overlap significantly or because, even outside their broadcast areas, the relatively weak signal from station X may still be strong enough to interfere with a signal from a distant station Y that is supposed to serve that area. There are occasionally other constraints as well governing stations that may be on different channels. For example, it may sometimes be forbidden to assign station X to channel 26 and station Y to channel 27 or 28.

For the incentive auction, let A denote the set of stations that choose to remain on-air and not to participate in the auction. It is always necessary to assign channels to those stations. In addition, there will be another set of stations R whose current bids the system would like to consider rejecting, because the prices demanded are too high. Combining these two groups, the set of stations that remain on-air if these bidders are rejected would be $S = A \cup R$. Before the auction system can decide to reject the bids of the stations in R, it must make sure that it is feasible to find channels for all the stations in S.

To study that problem, here is some additional notation. For each station $s \in S$, let $C(s)$ denote the set of channels potentially available to s, and let $C = \cup_{s \in S} C(s)$ be the set of all potentially available channels. Translated into words, this means a channel assignment is feasible if every station in S is assigned to an acceptable channel and if no pair of stations is assigned in a manner that is excluded by interference constraints. A channel assignment is a mapping $c : S \rightarrow C$.

Formally, the channel assignment c is *feasible* if (i) for all stations $s \in S$, $c(s) \in C(s)$ and (ii) for every pair of stations $(s, s') \in S \times S$, $\big((s, c(s)), (s', c(s'))\big) \notin X$, where X is the set of excluded pairs. Recall that N is the full set of stations. The collection of sets of stations that can feasibly be rejected is obtained from the feasible channel assignments, as follows:

$$\mathcal{R} = \big\{ R \subseteq N - A \mid (\exists c : A \cup R \rightarrow C) \\ c \text{ is a feasible channel assignment} \big\}.$$

Notice that $\mathcal{R}$ is a collection of sets of stations, which is defined by starting with a set of feasible channel assignments $\{s, c(s)\} \subseteq (A \cup R) \times C$, which is a set of pairs, and then taking just the station from each pair and including only stations in $N - A$. This is a complicated construction, and there is no guarantee that $\mathcal{R}$ must have any particularly nice structure. And yet, in many cases, it does have a nice structure.

For example, if there are just fifteen channels available to use in some metropolitan area, then the total number of stations assigned to continue broadcasting in that area must not exceed fifteen. If metropolitan areas were separated and these were the only interference constraints, then this set of constraints would define a matroid.

As another example, suppose that it is always possible to find a feasible channel assignment c for any set of stations S that do not have too many interference constraints among them in total, say no more than I. If s_n is the number of interference constraints involving station n, then a sufficient condition for feasibility of S would be that $\Sigma_{n \in S} s_n \leq I$, so that describes a knapsack problem. Harking back to our study of that problem, one could then find an approximate optimum by ranking the stations using v_n/s_n and packing greedily using that index.

In the actual FCC problem, either a knapsack constraint or a close-to-matroid constraint could be binding on the allocation, and which one is binding can affect whether the stations are better ranked by v_n (which can work very well in the event that $\mathcal{R}$ is nearly a matroid) or by v_n/s_n (which can work very well if the knapsack constraint is the binding one). Compromises are also possible. For example, one could rank stations according to $v_n/\sqrt{s_n}$, and something similar to that underlies the greedy algorithm used in the FCC's incentive auction.

5

CONCLUSION

In economic theory, the textbook approach to studying prices in competitive markets incorporates a variety of assumptions, two of which I emphasize in this monograph. The first is that resources can be fairly described as aggregates, ignoring many of the factors that tend to make individual goods unique. The second is the closely related assumption that the only relevant physical constraints on an allocation are the resource constraints. These are constraints of the form that one cannot allocate more of a good than the available supply. For example, when discussing air traffic through a major city airport, an economics textbook might treat the daily passenger capacity of the airport as limited. Then, to encourage efficient use, it may be desirable to charge airlines a fee per passenger, with the fee possibly varying between the most and least congested times of day to encourage airlines to avoid adding flights at the most congested times.

To flight controllers deciding which planes may take off and which may land, however, this high-level view is far from a complete account. The challenge is not just to ensure that the total passenger traffic during busy hours at an airport is appropriately limited but also to assign landing times, runways, and terminals to cope with the details of the flow. In transportation networks, constraints must be imposed to ensure that cars, planes, and trains do not crash, not merely to limit total traffic flow. Similarly, in allocating frequencies for broadcast television, it is not enough to limit the number of stations broadcasting in each city. Broadcasters also need to be assigned to channels in ways that avoid interference among their signals.

Some kinds of constraints are, in practice, handled differently for long-run and short-run planning. When a consumer flips on a light switch at 8:02 p.m., it does not help to have the power delivered at 8:04 p.m. In abstract economic theory, this sort of detail is brushed aside by a conceptual trick: one says that power at different times represents different products, and the consumer in this example demands one, but not the other. But this trick is of little use in a price-guided system for resource allocation, because it results in too many products and too many different prices. There is no practical way to design a power system with bids and prices that vary second by second or even minute by minute. In the long run, when power systems are planned, the planner may ask about what overall peak capacity needs to be, but in the short run, when power is delivered, every detail of where and when looms as important. The practical consequence is that even in power systems featuring markets, the products are not second-by-second or location-by-location power. Instead, much more coarsely defined products are used, and a centralized system operator imposes decisions on the market participants to fill in the details that the bids in the market do not decide.

This monograph attempts to bridge some of the gap between detailed engineering models, which are often used to dispatch resources in the short run, and the possibility of using prices and auctions to guide resource allocation. It is important in economic analysis that if prices help to guide short-run allocations, then those same prices should provide good investment incentives for long-run capacity decisions. Much of chapter 3 was devoted to an analysis of that nexus.

Another set of questions concerns when prices can be used, even in principle, to guide efficient short-run decisions. Often, they cannot be used. Short-run allocation problems can be computationally hard, and prices that support efficient decisions may not even exist. That is why another theme of this monograph has been about the use of auctions. As we have seen, when goods are exactly substitutes, then prices to clear markets do exist and can be found using ascending auctions. The new finding is that when goods are approximately substitutes—a condition that my analysis measures and makes precise—there are ascending auctions that lead to approximately efficient allocations. Moreover, these auctions have some especially nice properties. As explained in chapter 4, they can be group strategy-proof, obviously strategy-proof, and privacy preserving for winning bidders.

Analyses of this kind are new, and as this text is being written, the massive application of some of these ideas in the design of the FCC broadcast incentive auction is testing their value. If successful, applications of this kind may set a standard for other hard resource-allocation problems in transportation and other sectors.

NOTES

1. INTRODUCTION

1. According to U.S. Wheat Associates (http://www.uswheat.org/wheatGrade), number 2 red wheat is wheat that does not qualify as number 1 and yet weighs at least 58 pounds per bushel; includes no more than 4 percent damaged kernels, including not more than 0.2 percent suffering heat damage; has no more than 0.7 percent foreign material, 5 percent shrunken and broken kernels, 5 percent wheat from other classes (such as white wheat), or 2 percent wheat from contrasting classes; and no more than 5 percent total defects (which includes damaged kernels [total], foreign material, and shrunken and broken kernels).
2. Another problem with the neoclassical model is that when products are defined very finely far too many prices are required. Much of the attraction of the model is that just a few prices for individual items can guide complex decisions involving multiple items. For example, for an air traffic control problem, the constraint that two planes do not crash could be stated as a resource constraint, treating each minute and cubic meter of space as a separate resource. A flight plan uses a particular set of these resources, and a set of flight plans

is consistent if the total demand for any one resource does not exceed 1. This is a logically coherent formulation, but adjusting individual resource prices in an attempt to find an optimal set of flight plans would not be likely to succeed. As I will demonstrate later, prices are much more effective for guiding substitution among resources than for guiding the use of complementary resources of the kind used by flight plans.

3. Photographs of several nail houses can be found at www.oddee.com/item_99288.aspx.
4. Record keeping is an issue in modern market design as well. One of the first steps in setting up a successful kidney exchange was to create a database of patients and donors and their characteristics (Roth et al. 2005).
5. In the early days of television, the channels on a TV receiver corresponded to physical frequency bands. Today, however, the channel number that a viewer specifies on his or her TV may be different from the frequency channel used to carry any over-the-air broadcast. It is the physical channels in the UHF range that have become valuable for wireless broadband uses, not the virtual channels that consumers select when they choose a station using their cable or satellite service.
6. For example, constraints are imposed by treaties with Canada and Mexico that limit the ways certain channels can be used. Besides the cochannel constraints, the treaty restrictions prevent certain pairs of stations from being assigned to channel numbers that differ by two or less, providing additional protection against interference. These constraints do not exactly match those of a standard graph-coloring problem. Canada has agreed to reassign its own TV stations to clear the same frequencies as those in the United States, and to coordinate the reassignment. This will benefit both countries, allowing a full clearing of frequencies in the United States and allowing Canada to use the same frequencies for mobile broadband as those to be used in the United States. Mexico has also agreed

to keep certain frequencies clear of TV broadcasts, but only for TV channels 38–51.

7. NP-complete problems are thought to be impossible to solve with a "fast" algorithm. For graph coloring, a fast algorithm would be one for which the solution time for a graph with N arcs is bounded by $\alpha N^{\alpha+1}$ for some positive number α. If an algorithm is not fast in this sense, then no such α exists; so for every α, there are some problems for which the algorithm takes time per arc of more than αN^{α}. In practice, this means that the algorithm is likely to take an impractically long time on at least some hard problems of large size.
8. Low-powered broadcasters—so-called LPTV stations—were not given this right. Their licenses had specified that their rights were secondary ones, allowing them to broadcast on a frequency only if it did not create interference with the primary uses, and the new mobile broadband licenses were to become the new primary uses.
9. My colleague Stanford economics professor Robert Wilson and I invented the activity rule in 1993 as part of our suggested "simultaneous multiple-round auction." According to an activity rule, bidder's activity in placing new bids or maintaining their high bids is measured at each round of the auction. If a bidder is not sufficiently active, then it loses some of its eligibility to bid in future rounds of the auction. The first activity rule was incorporated into the first U.S. spectrum auctions in 1994, and similar rules have been part of every U.S. spectrum auction since that time, as well as nearly every spectrum auction worldwide.

2. (NEAR-)SUBSTITUTES, PRICES, AND STABILITY

1. In contrast, Arrow and Hurwicz proved that, for their model, there is a unique market-clearing price vector. There are two differences between their model and the one presented here

that account for this difference. First, in the Arrow-Hurwicz model, market-clearing includes the condition that there is zero net demand for the numeraire good, whereas the model presented here only requires market clearing for a limited set of goods. Second, their model assumes that all goods, not just the nonnumeraire goods, are gross substitutes. That extra assumption implies that given any two price vectors for the nonnumeraire goods, with one vector larger than the other in every component, the net demand for the numeraire good must be strictly greater at the higher price vector. So, the two price vectors cannot both clear the market for the numeraire good. Hence, in their model, there can be just one market-clearing price vector.

2. Even with more than two nonnumeraire goods, there are highest and lowest equilibrium price vectors. Proof is omitted here.
3. Kelso and Crawford develop the theory without the extra assumption that firms are never indifferent between sets of workers. Without that assumption, a firm's demand is described by a multivalued demand function $D^j(\cdot)$, where $D^j(w^j)$ is a collection of sets of workers, each of which is an optimal choice for the firm at wage vector w^j. (For almost all wage vectors w^j, $D^j(w)$ will be a singleton, but exceptions are inevitable when firms are profit maximizers and the full set of prices is considered.) With this formulation, workers are *gross substitutes* for a firm with demand D^j if, for any two vectors of wages $w^j \leq w'^j$ (meaning that each component of w'^j is weakly larger than the corresponding component of w^j), if $T \subset S \in D^j(w^j)$ and $w_i^j = w_i'^j$ for all $i \in T$, then there is some S' such that $T \subseteq S' \in D^j(w'^j)$.

Informally, this definition of substitutes has just the same interpretation as the special case of single-valued demand functions defined only on the restricted wage domain W. It says that raising wages for some workers never diminishes the demand for the group of workers (those in T) whose wages remain unchanged.

4. Notice that if $j \in R_i(w)$, then $i \in D^j(w^j)$, which implies that there is some $n \leq N$ such that $w_i^j = \hat{w}_n$. Hence, the values specified for F are in the proper range.
5. For inequalities among vectors in $\mathbb{R}^N$, we write $x \leq y$ to mean $x_n \leq y_n$ for $n = 1, \ldots, N$; $x < y$ to mean $x \leq y$ and $x \neq y$; and $x \ll y$ to mean $x_n < y_n$ for $n = 1, \ldots, N$.
6. Operations researchers and computer scientists have characterized just how hard this class of problems can be as part of a branch of mathematics known as *complexity theory*. The problem of *checking* whether a proposed solution $\hat{x}$ to a knapsack problem is optimal is NP-complete (Papadimitriou, 1994). This characterization of "hardness" is usually understood against the background of the common complexity theory hypothesis that $P \neq NP$. With this hypothesis, the statement that the class of knapsack problems is NP-complete means that for *any* solution algorithm and *any* polynomial function F, there are knapsack problems whose run times are longer than $F(N)$. An informal way to describe this conclusion is to say that knapsack problems have "exponential" worst-case run times.
7. In cases in which two items have the same value/size, one can use randomization to break the tie and fix an ordering.
8. If a firm is a profit maximizer in this model and workers are substitutes, then one can show that increasing a wage cannot increase the number of workers the firm hires. This property, known as the "law of aggregate demand," was established by Hatfield and Milgrom (2005).
9. The assumption that a bidder knows what the item is worth is not an innocent one for many auctions, since some items derive value based on things like perceived beauty or authenticity or resale value that may depend on what others know.

Those can be important issues, but they are not the main issues for this monograph, so we assume throughout that bidders do know their own values.

10. Here is the proof. If $\alpha(v)$ is *not* monotonic, that means there is some v such that $n \in \alpha(v)$ and some $v'_n > v_n$ such that $n \notin \alpha(v'_n, v_{-n})$. In that case, one of the types v_n or v'_n must have an incentive to misreport when the others have type profile v_{-n}. For if type v_n has no such incentive, then $v_n - p_n(v) \geq p_n(v'_n, v_{-n})$. In that case, if n's type is v'_n and he or she misreports his or her type to be v_n, he or she wins and gets the payoff $v'_n - p_n(v) > v_n - p_n(v) \geq p_n(v'_n, v_{-n})$. In other words, the payoff from misreporting is strictly higher than the payoff from reporting truthfully.
11. One can also define a *mixed* Nash equilibrium in a similar way, by allowing the owners to randomize among their pure strategies. We have not used that in our model, so we omit it here.
12. The law of demand applies in my specification, because the form of the players' payoffs eliminates any "income effect." The issue of income effects is developed in detail in many standard introductory texts in microeconomics.
13. At the cost of some extra notation, this can be extended to the case in which the buyer has a different value for each item that is to be subtracted from the cost in its cost-minimization problem.
14. In this application, the actual constraints are much more complex. We describe and analyze those in a later chapter.
15. There is a large mathematics literature about matroids, with applications in combinatorial optimization, network theory, coding theory, and more. Although I have tried to make this chapter self-contained, all of the results about matroids reported here are well known. For additional details about matroid theory, see Neel and Neudauer (2009) or Oxley (2011).

3. VICKREY AUCTIONS AND SUBSTITUTION

1. When we formulate maximization problems later, we will assume that solutions exist for which it will be sufficient that the choice is to be made from a finite set. Much of the development that follows also works without the finiteness assumption, provided there are other ways to ensure that the required maxima exist.
2. If the path-connectedness assumption is omitted, one can construct an example with multiple payment rules as follows: suppose that $N = 1$ and that there is a single good for sale. The one bidder has a supply cost for the good that is either zero or one (so the possible values do not form a path-connected set). Consider the direct mechanism in which the item is purchased only if the reported cost is less than one half, and in that case the price paid is a number $p(0) \in (0, 1)$. Every such price corresponds to a different strategy-proof direct mechanism, so there is no unique strategy-proof price in this example. For the same outcome function α, if the possible costs are given by $\theta_1 \in \Theta_1 = [0, 1]$, then the only price that makes (α, p^{α}) strategy-proof is $p^{\alpha}(\theta) = \frac{1}{2}$ for $\theta < \frac{1}{2}$, and $p^{\alpha}(\theta) = 0$ otherwise.
3. The dependence of the coalition value on the presence of the buyer is suppressed in this notation, which makes it different from the usual textbook definition of the coalition-value function.

4. DEFERRED-ACCEPTANCE AUCTIONS AND NEAR-SUBSTITUTES

1. In auction design generally, nothing is more important than attracting bids from serious bidders. In the context of the incentive auction, a small business that owns a single TV

station in one or a few broadcast markets would likely be an inexperienced bidder facing very high stakes—selling the family business!—and engaging in an unfamiliar, once-in-a-lifetime transaction. After the auction, with fewer channels in operation, bidders who do not sell their rights would be assigned valuable channels. According to equilibrium theory, the prices paid in the auction might be close to the value of the channel after the auction, so nonparticipation could be a real and viable option for bidders. The best way to counter that incentive is to make participation in the auction safe and easy, especially for smaller bidders.

2. Readers seeking a formal, general account are referred to Li (2015).
3. Developments in this section are based on a paper by Milgrom and Segal (2015).
4. For example, we may restrict the decrements so that $\Delta(A^t) \geq \min\left(p_{n^*}(A^{t-1}), \underline{\Delta}\right)$ for some $\underline{\Delta} > 0$.

REFERENCES

Arrow, K. J., and L. Hurwicz. 1959. "On the Stability of the Competitive Equilibrium, II." *Econometrica* 27(1): 82–109.

Ausubel, Lawrence, and Paul Milgrom. 2002. "Ascending Auctions with Package Bidding." *Frontiers of Theoretical Economics* 1(1): article 1.

——. 2006. "The Lovely but Lonely Vickrey Auction." In *Combinatorial Auctions*, ed. P. Cramton, Y. Shoham, and R. Steinberg. Cambridge, MA: MIT Press.

Bleakley, Hoyt, and Joseph Ferrie. 2014. "Land Openings on the Georgia Frontier and the Coase Theorem in the Short-and Long-Run." Working paper.

Clarke, Edward H. 1971. "Multipart Pricing of Public Goods." *Public Choice* 11(1): 17–33.

Dantzig, George B. 1957. "Discrete-Variable Extremum Problems." *Operations Research* 5(2): 266–88.

Eilat, Assaf, and Paul Milgrom. 2011. "The CAF Auction: Design Proposal." WC Docket No. 10-90 et al., filed July 29, 2011.

Fudenberg, Drew, and Jean Tirole. 1991. *Game Theory*. Cambridge, MA: MIT Press.

Green, Jerry, and Jean-Jacques Laffont. 1977. "Characterization of Satisfactory Mechanisms for the Revelation of Preferences for Public Goods." *Econometrica* 45(2): 427–38.

Groves, Theodore. 1973. "Incentives in Teams." *Econometrica* 41(4): 617–31.

Hatfield, John W., and Paul Milgrom. 2005. "Matching with Contracts." *American Economic Review* 95(4): 913–35.

Holmström, Bengt. 1979. "Groves' Scheme on Restricted Domains." *Econometrica* 47(5): 1137–44.

Kagel, J. H., R. M. Harstad, and Dan Levin. 1987. "Information Impact and Allocation Rules in Auctions with Affiliated Private Values: A Laboratory Study." *Econometrica* 55(6): 1275–1304.

Kagel, J. H., and Dan Levin. 1993. "Independent Private Value Auctions: Bidder Behaviour in First-, Second-, and Third-Price Auctions with Varying Numbers of Bidders." *Economic Journal* 103: 868–79.

Karp, Richard M. 1975. "Reducibility Among Combinatorial Problems." *Journal of Symbolic Logic* 40(4): 618–19.

Kelso, Alexander Jr. and Vincent Crawford. 1982. "Job Matching, Coalition Formation, and Gross Substitutes." *Econometrica* 50(6): 1483–1504.

Lehmann, D., L. I. O'Callaghan, and Yoav Shoham. 2002. "Truth Revelation in Approximately Efficient Combinatorial Auctions." *Journal of the ACM* 49(5): 577–602.

Leyton-Brown, Kevin, Paul Milgrom, Neil Newman, and Ilya Segal. 2016. "Simulating Economic Outcomes in Reverse Clock Auctions for Radio Spectrum." Working paper.

Li, Shengwu. 2015. "Obviously Strategy-Proof Mechanisms." Working Paper. https://ssrn.com/abstract=2560028.

Milgrom, Paul. 2000. "Putting Auction Theory to Work: The Simultaneous Ascending Auction." *Journal of Political Economy* 108(2): 245–72.

——. 2004. *Putting Auction Theory to Work*. Cambridge, U.K.: Cambridge University Press.

——. 2009. "Assignment Messages and Exchanges." *American Economic Journal: Miocroeconomics* 1(2): 95–113.

Milgrom, Paul, and Ilya Segal. 2002. "Envelope Theorems for Arbitrary Choice Sets." *Econometrica* 70(2): 583–601.

Milgrom, Paul, and Ilya Segal. 2015. "Deferred-Acceptance Auctions and Radio Spectrum Reallocation." Working Paper.

Milgrom, Paul, and Bruno Strulovici. 2009. "Substitute Goods, Auctions, and Equilibrium." *Journal of Economic Theory* 144(1): 212–47.

Nash, John F. 1950. "Equilibrium Points in *n*-Person Games." *Proceedings of the National Academy of Sciences of the United States of America* 36(1): 48–49.

Neel, David, and Nancy Neudauer. 2009. "Matroids You Have Known," *Mathematics Magazine* 82(1): 26–41.

Oxley, James. 2011. *Matroid Theory*, 2nd edition. Oxford, U.K.: Oxford University Press.

Papadimitriou, Christos H. 1994. *Computational Complexity*. Reading, MA: Addison-Wesley.

Roth, Alvin, Tayfun Sönmez, and Utku Ünver. 2005. "A Kidney Exchange Clearinghouse in New England." *AEA Papers and Proceedings* 95(2): 376–80.

Rothkopf, M. H., T. J. Teisberg, and E. P. Kahn. 1990. "Why Are Vickrey Auctions Rare?" *Journal of Political Economy* 98(1): 94–109.

Smith, Adam. 1776. *An Inquiry into the Nature and Causes of the Wealth of Nations.* London: Methuen and Co, Ltd.

Vickrey, William. 1961. "Counterspeculation, Auctions, and Competitive Sealed Tenders." *Journal of Finance* 16(1):8–37.

Walras, Léon. 1874. *Elements of Pure Economics*. London: Routledge.

INDEX

Page numbers in italics represent tables or figures

CPSIA information can be obtained
at www.ICGtesting.com
Printed in the USA
LVHW110933250221
679407LV00006BB/6